FLAMINGO FLAMETTI

Tal R
Harpune Wien
Axel Heil

VERLAG FÜR MODERNE KUNST

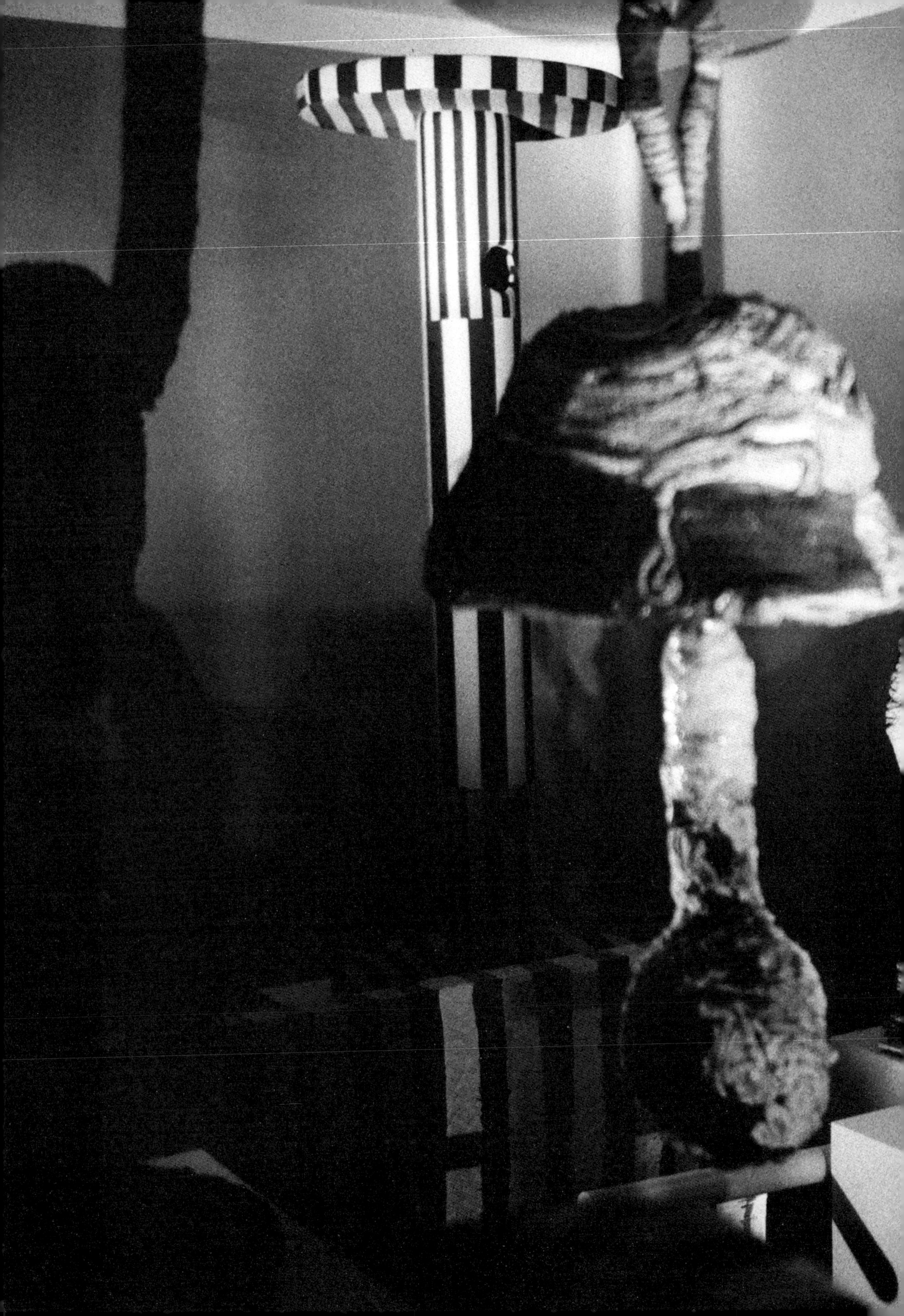

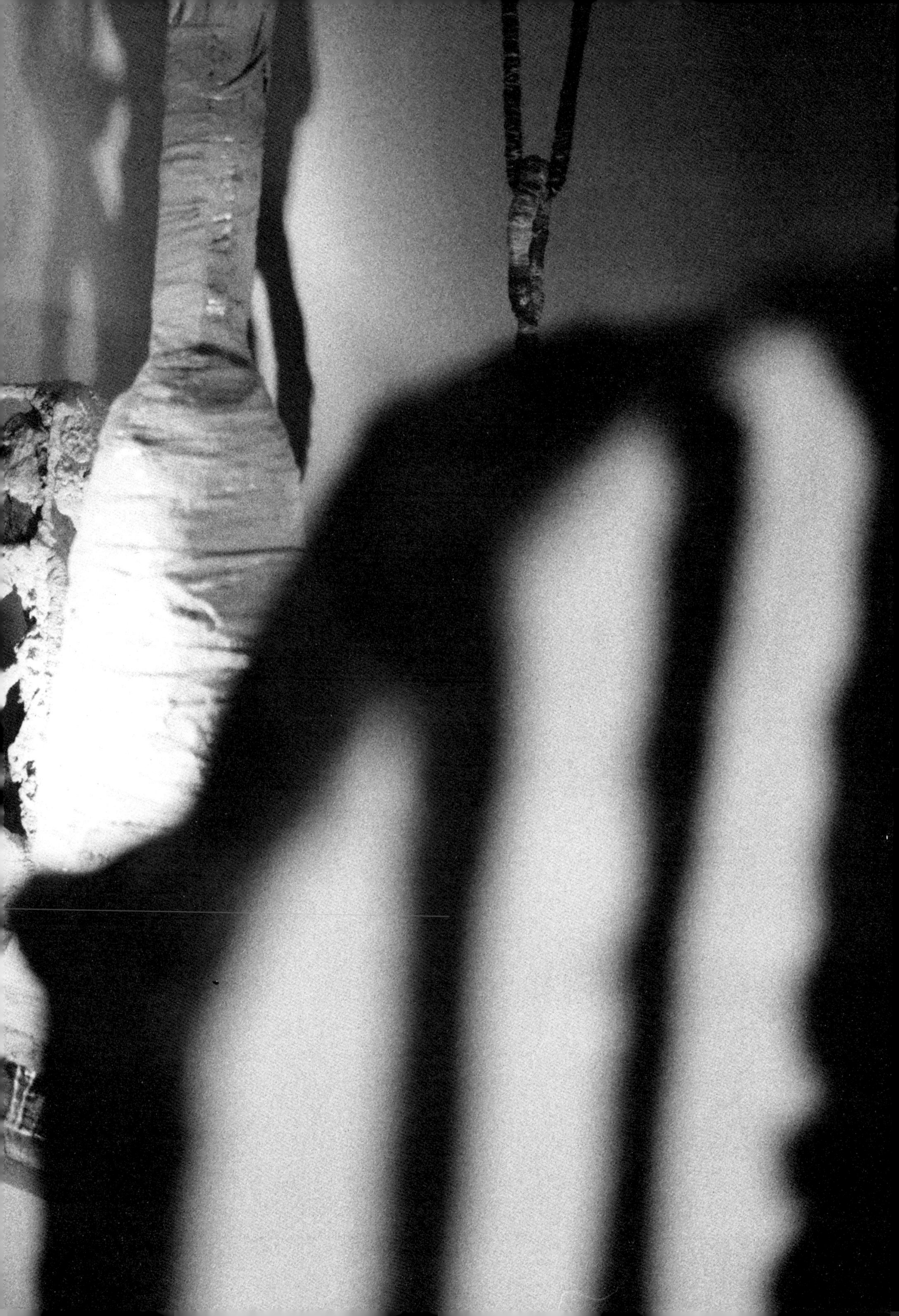

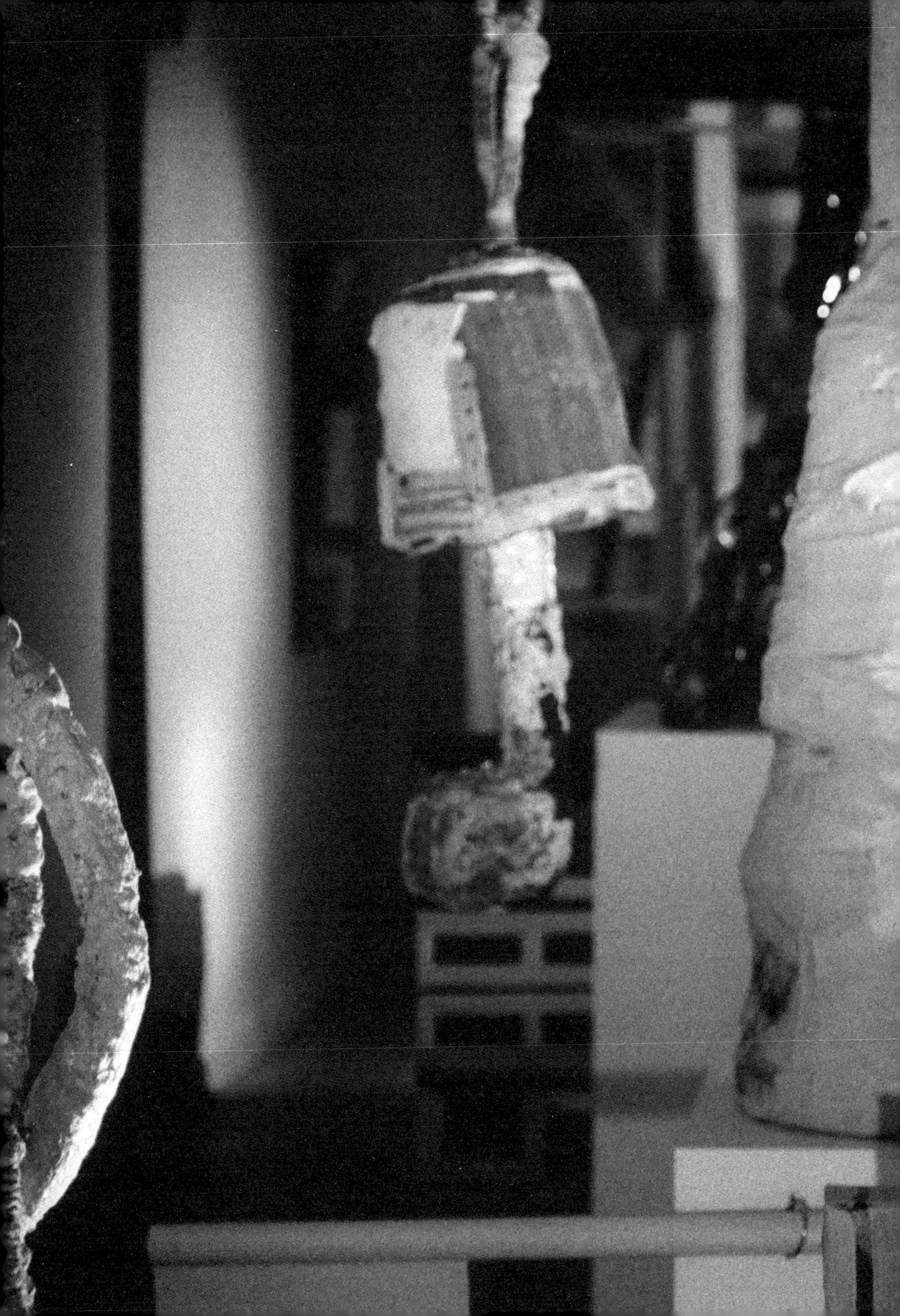

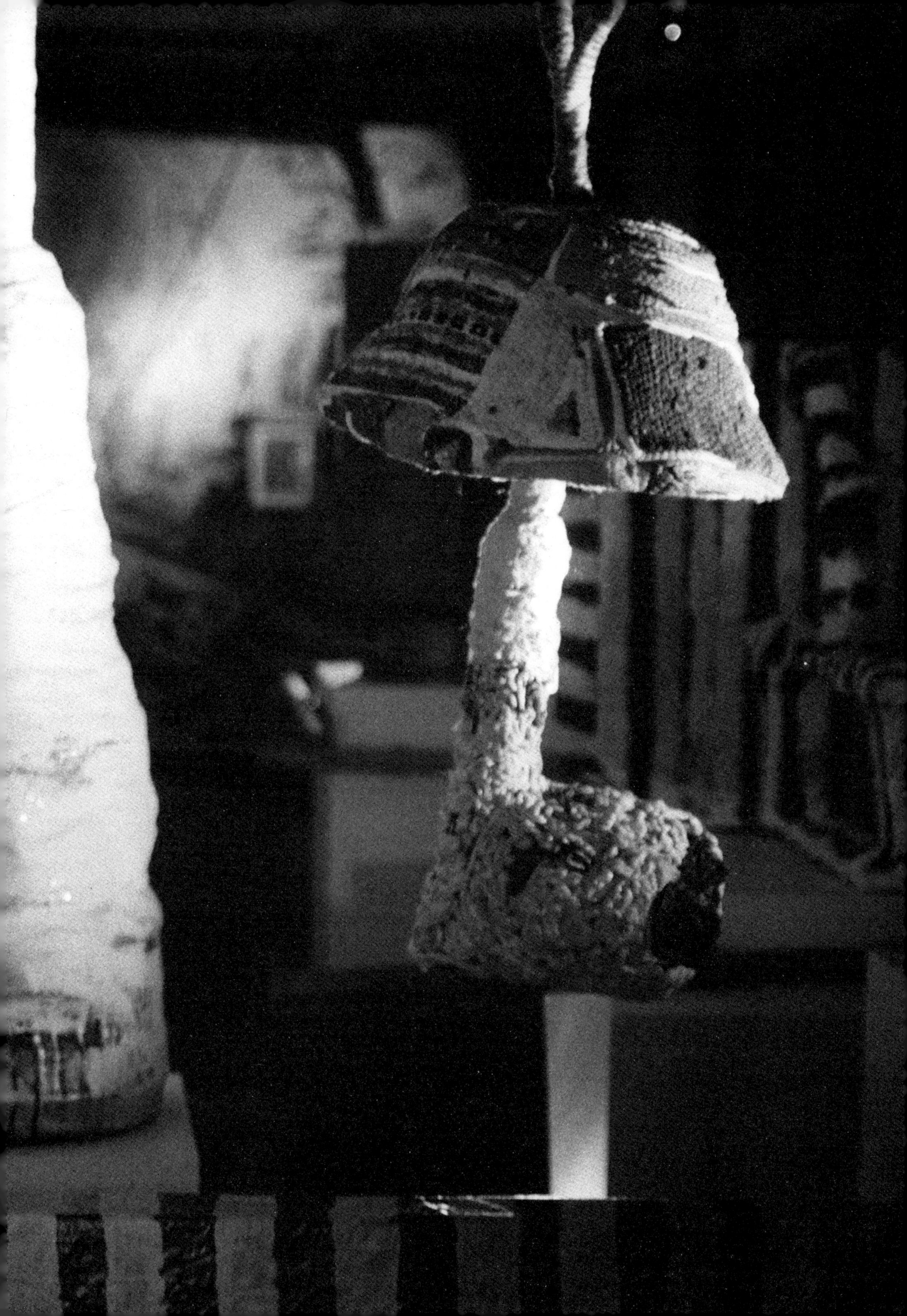

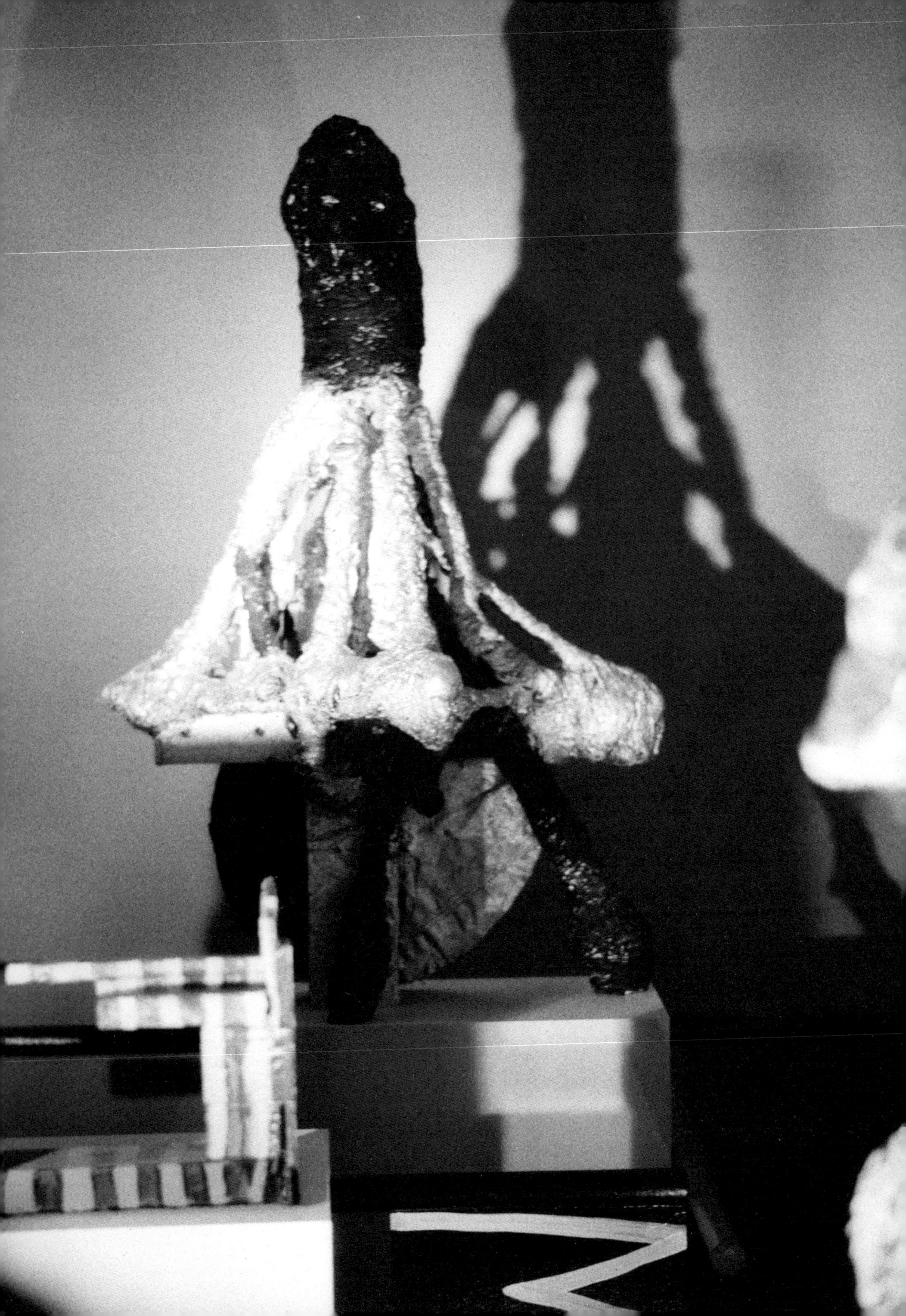

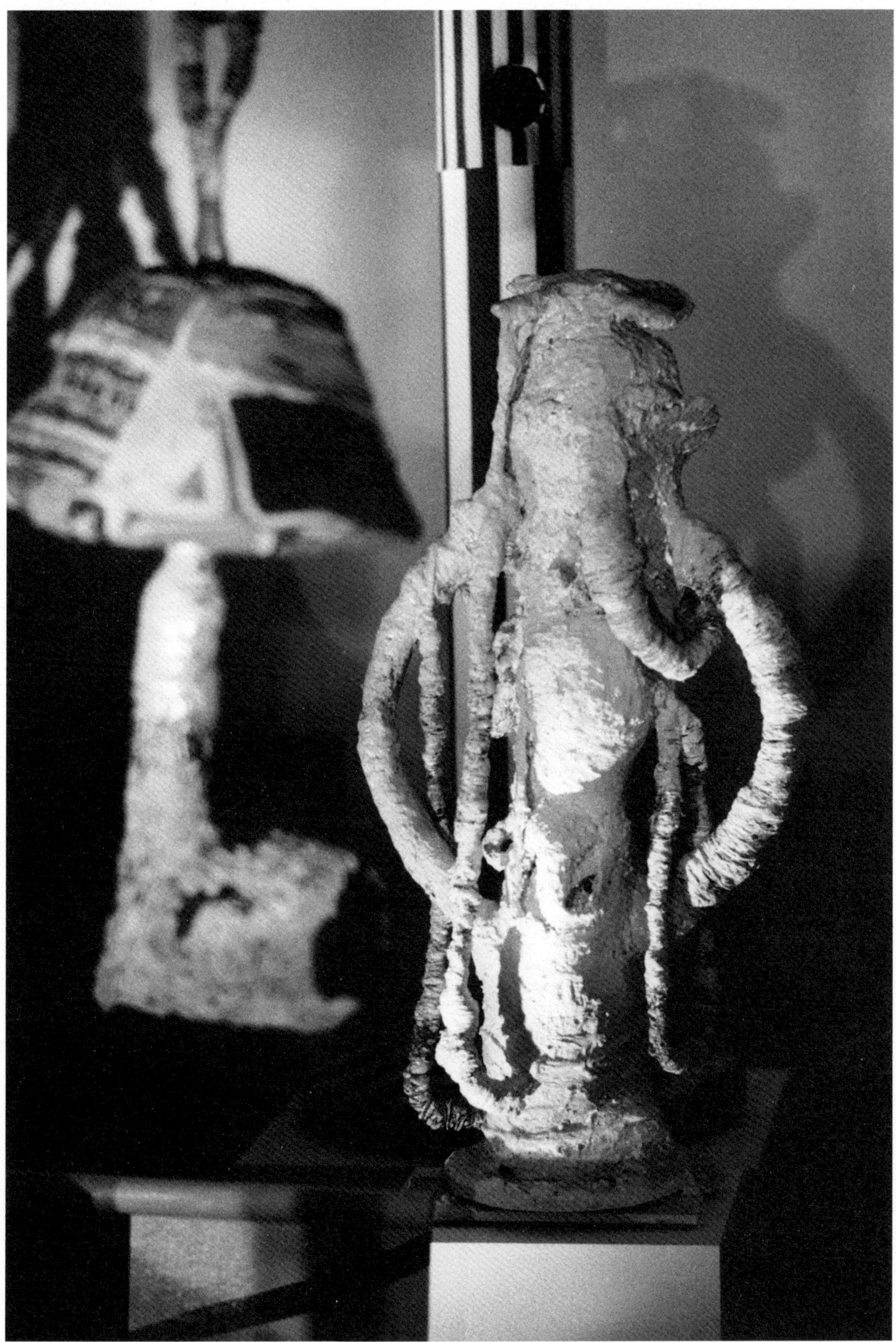

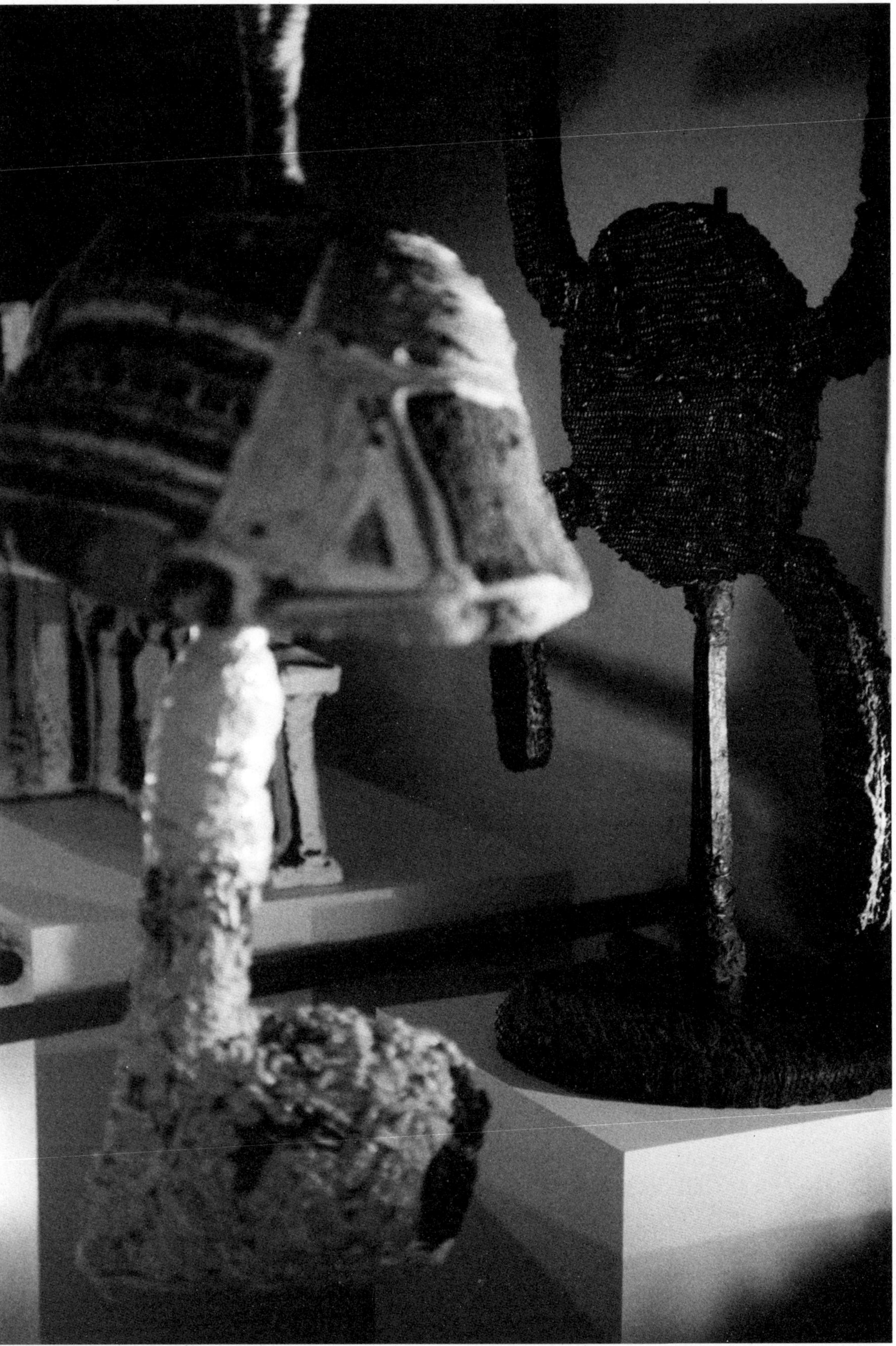

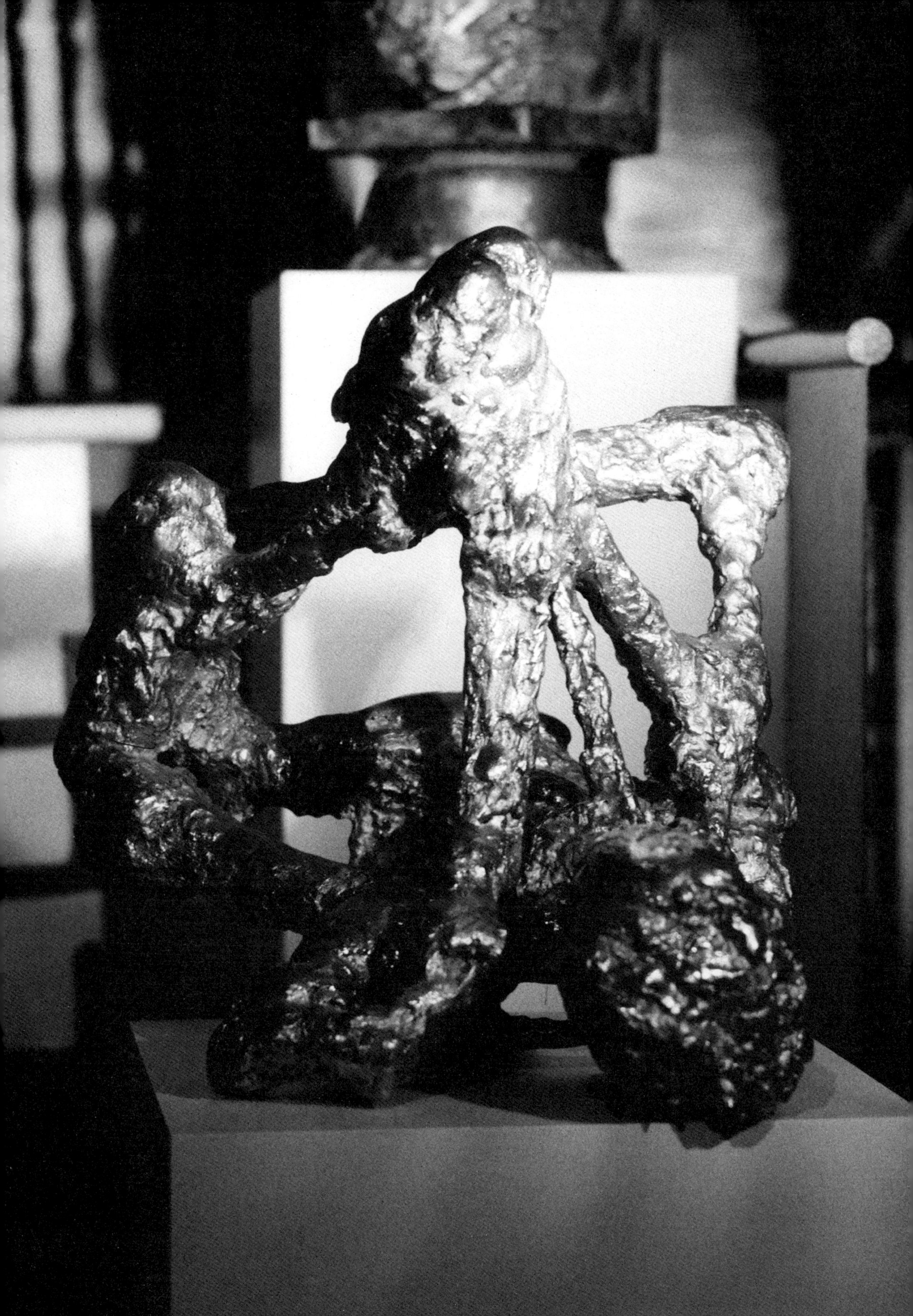

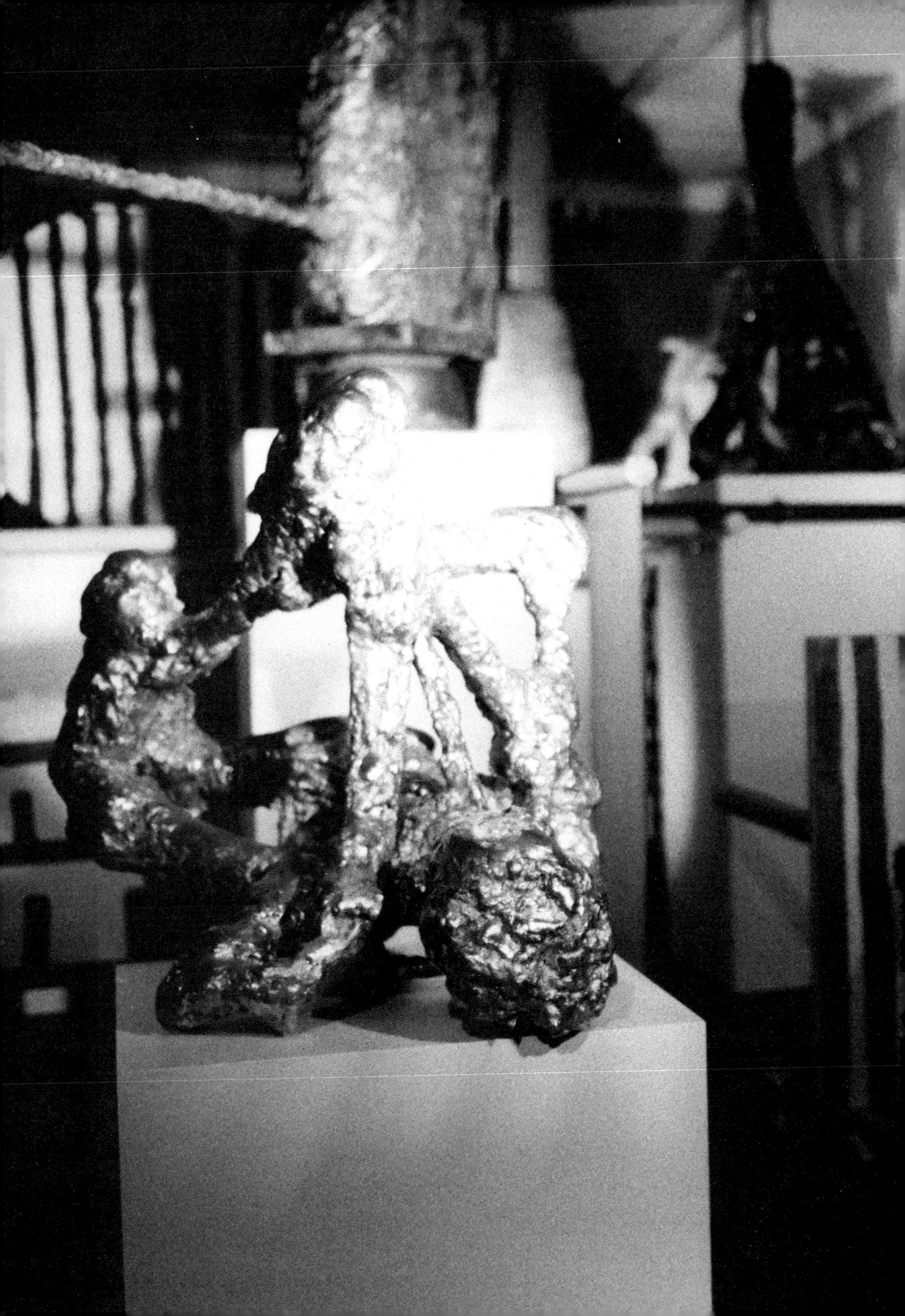

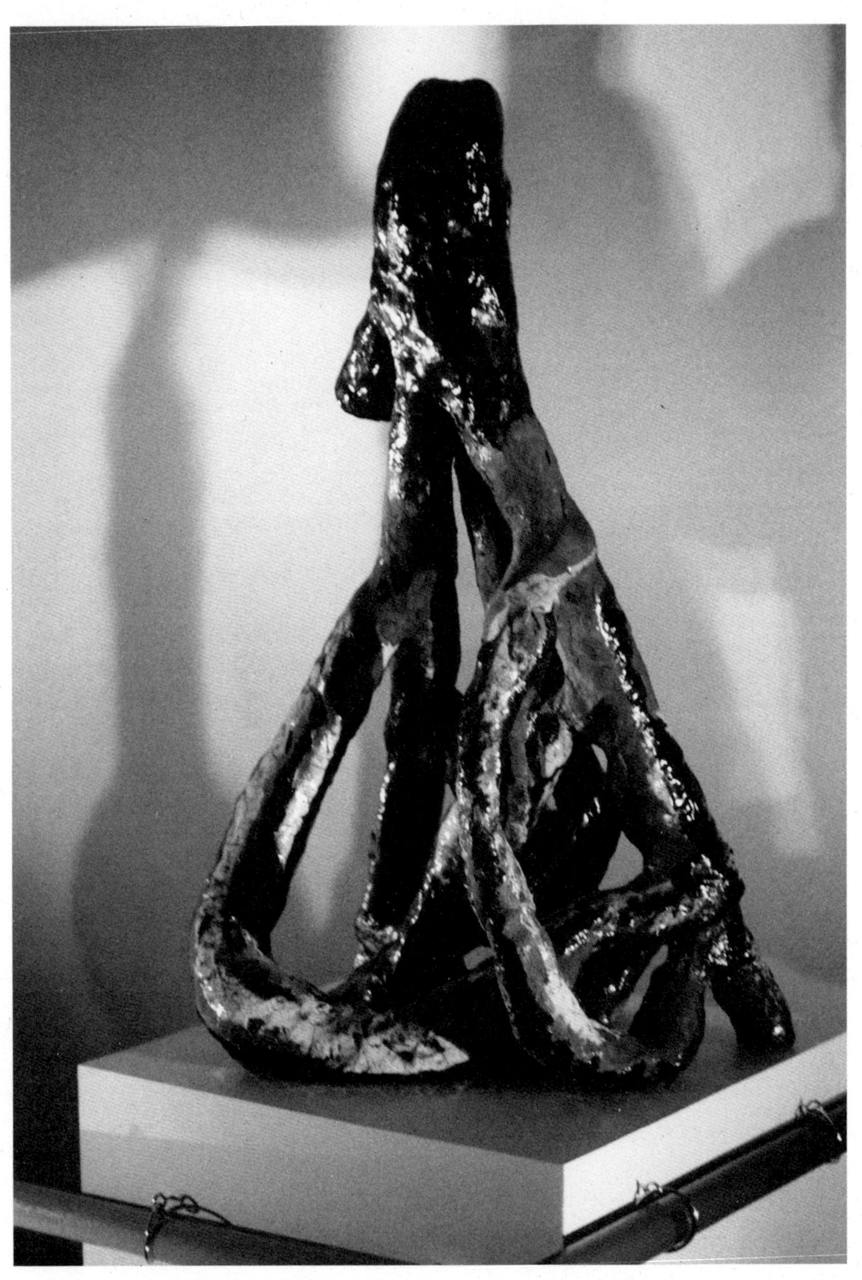

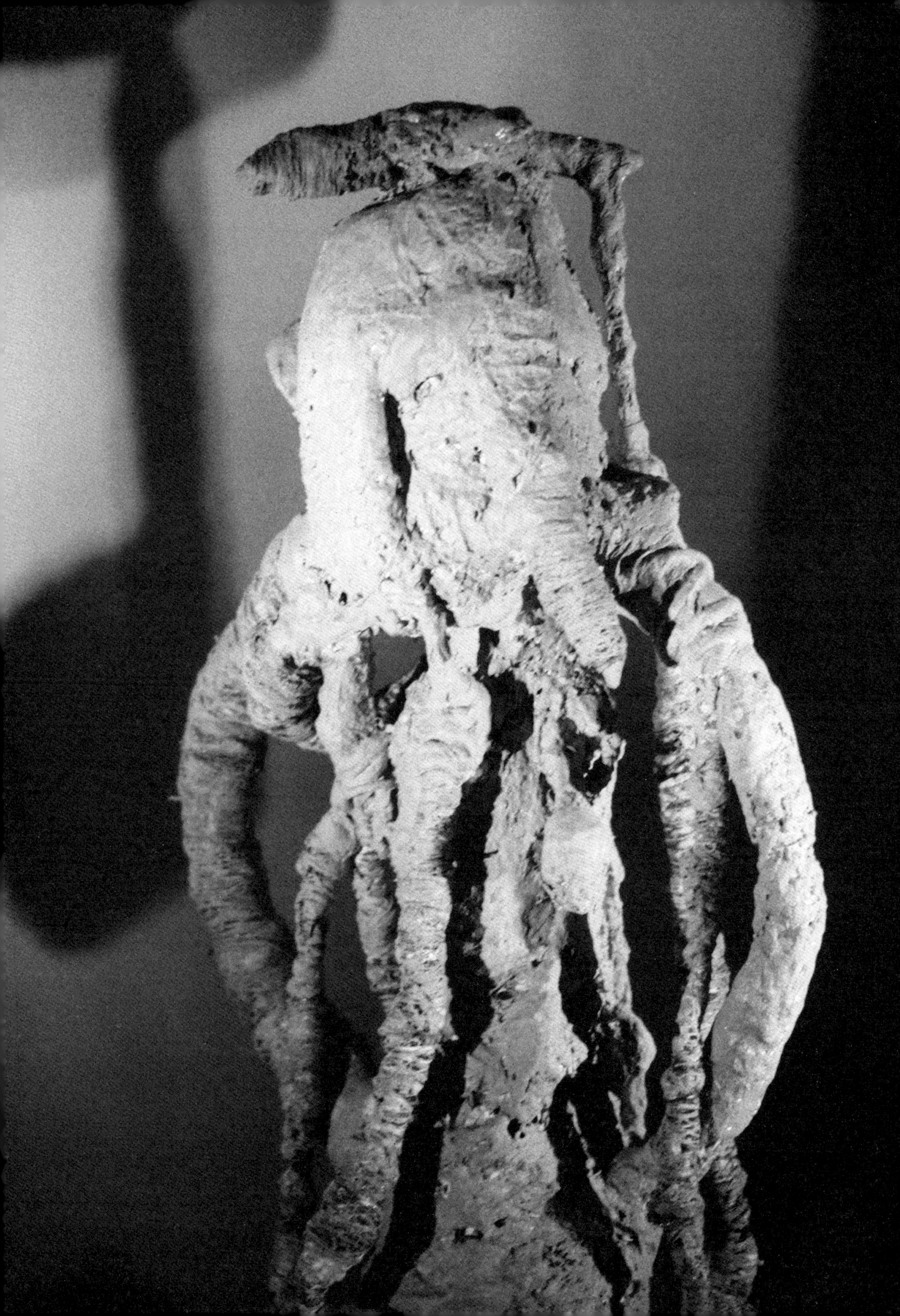

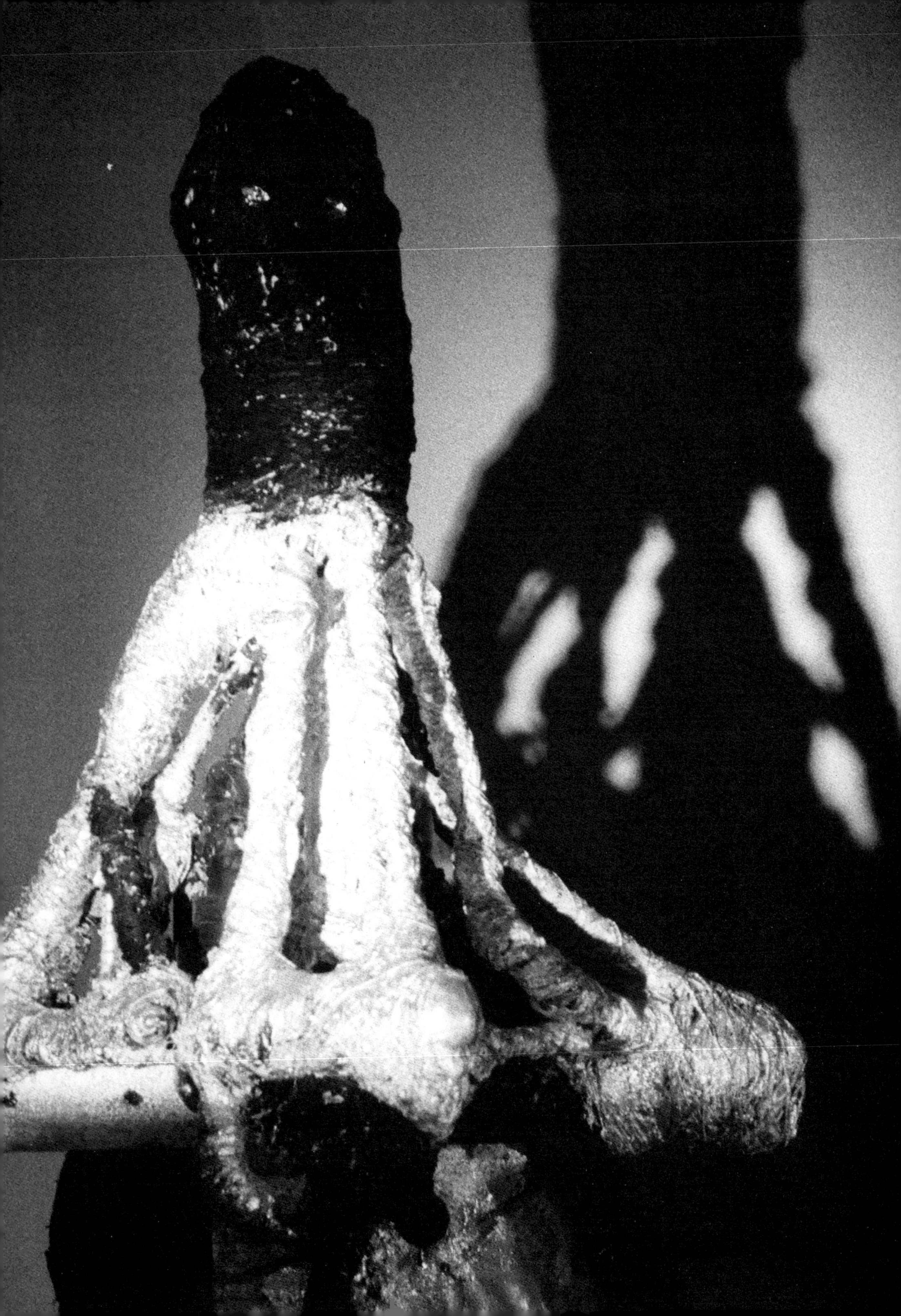

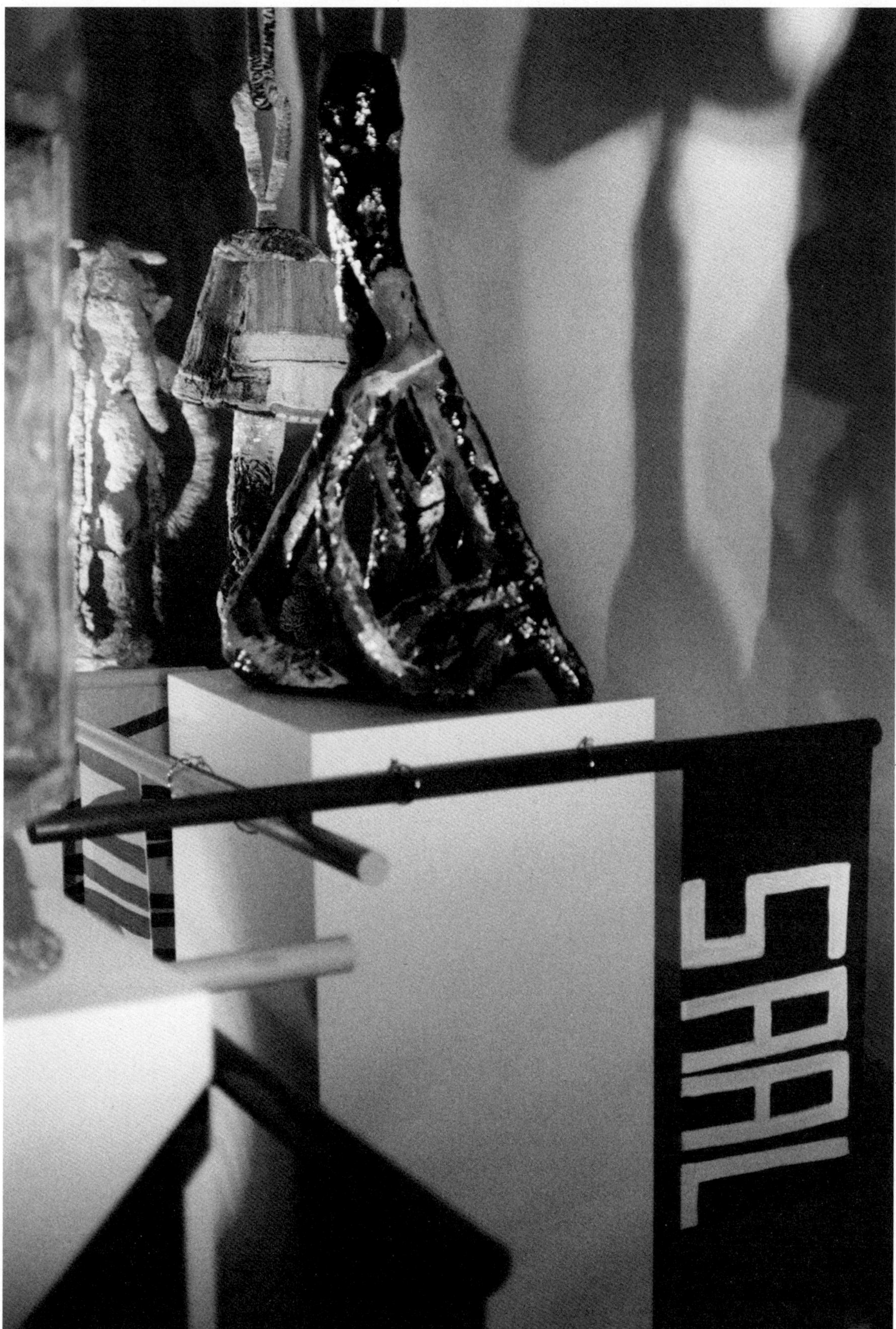

SAAL

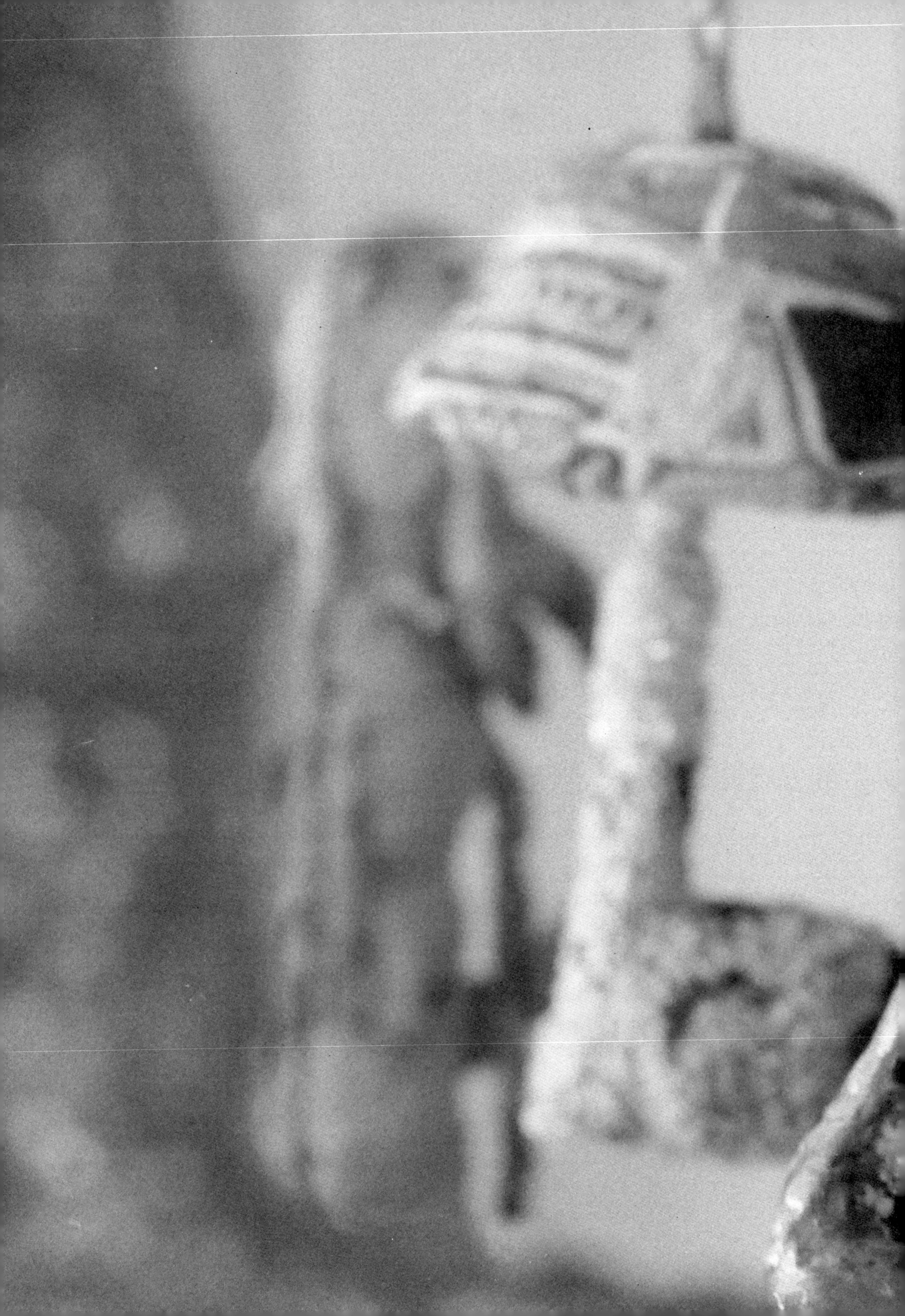

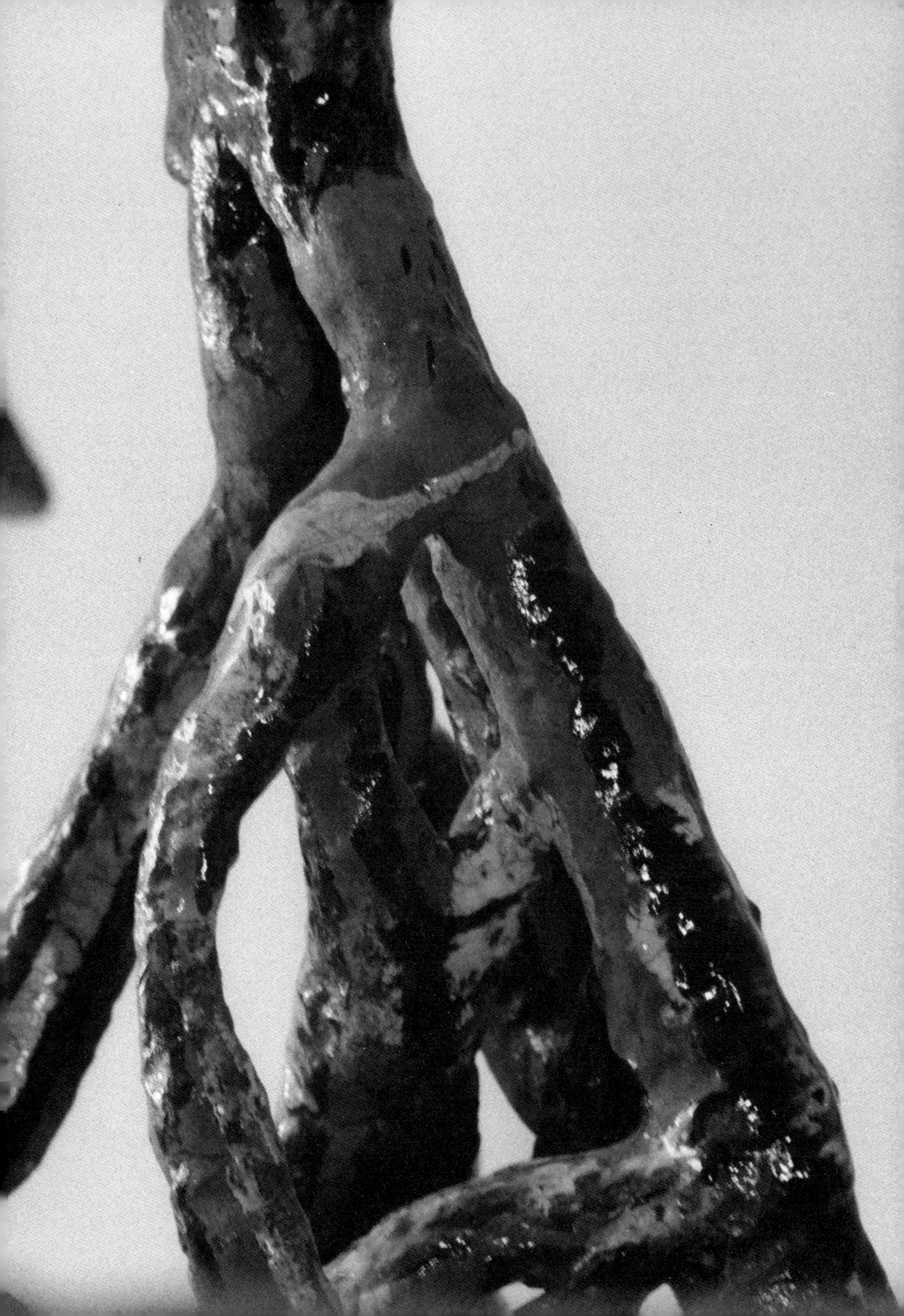

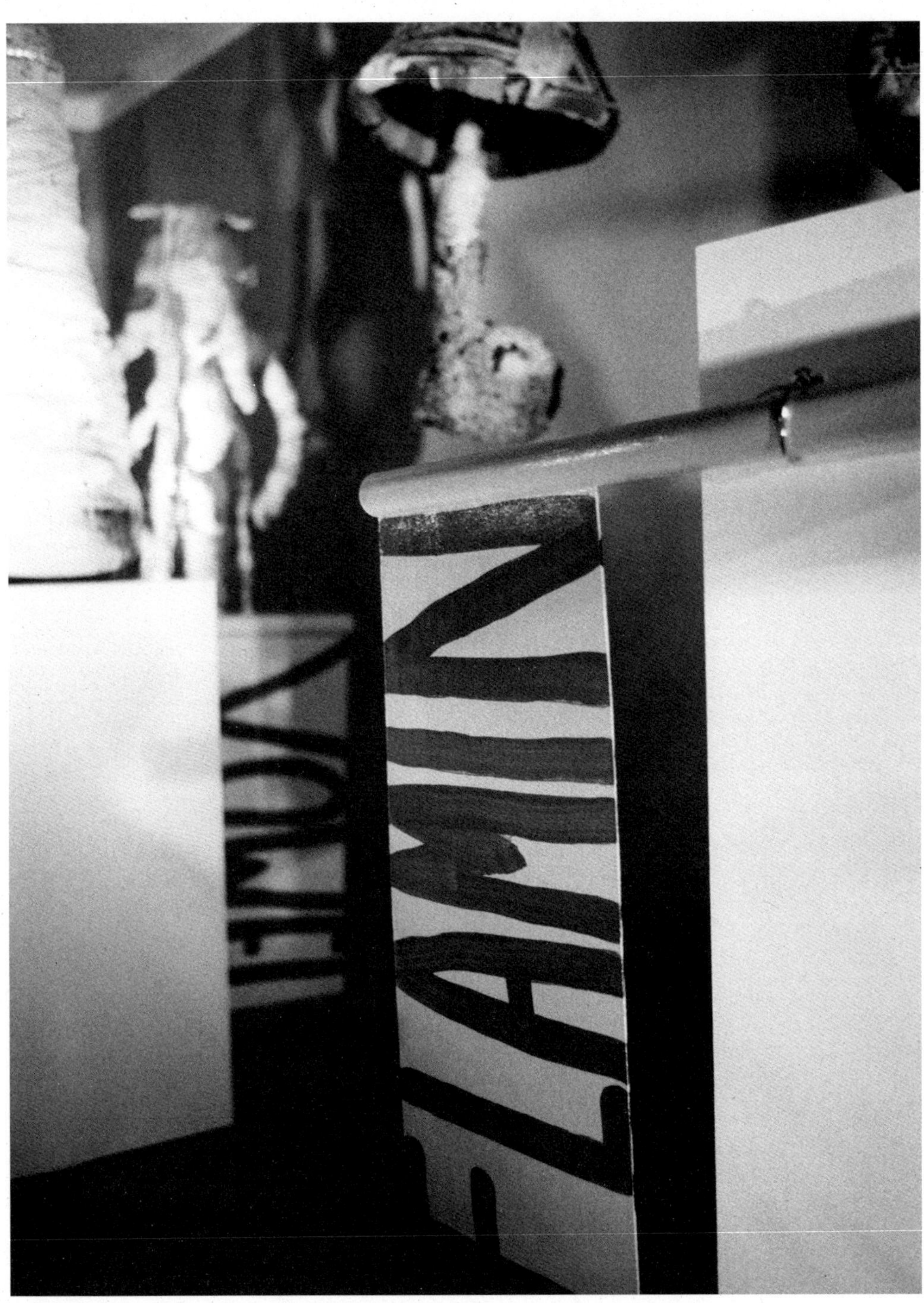

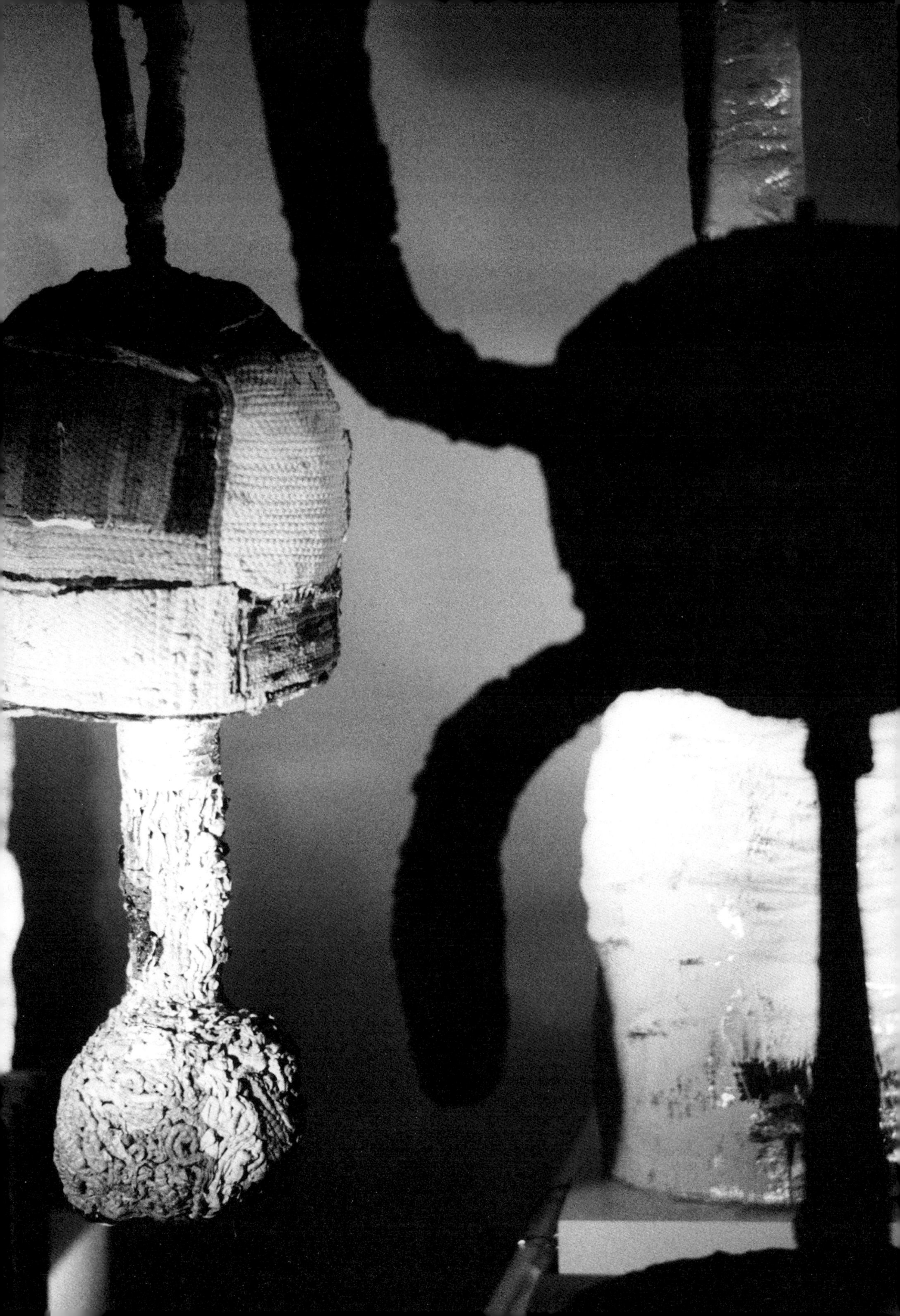

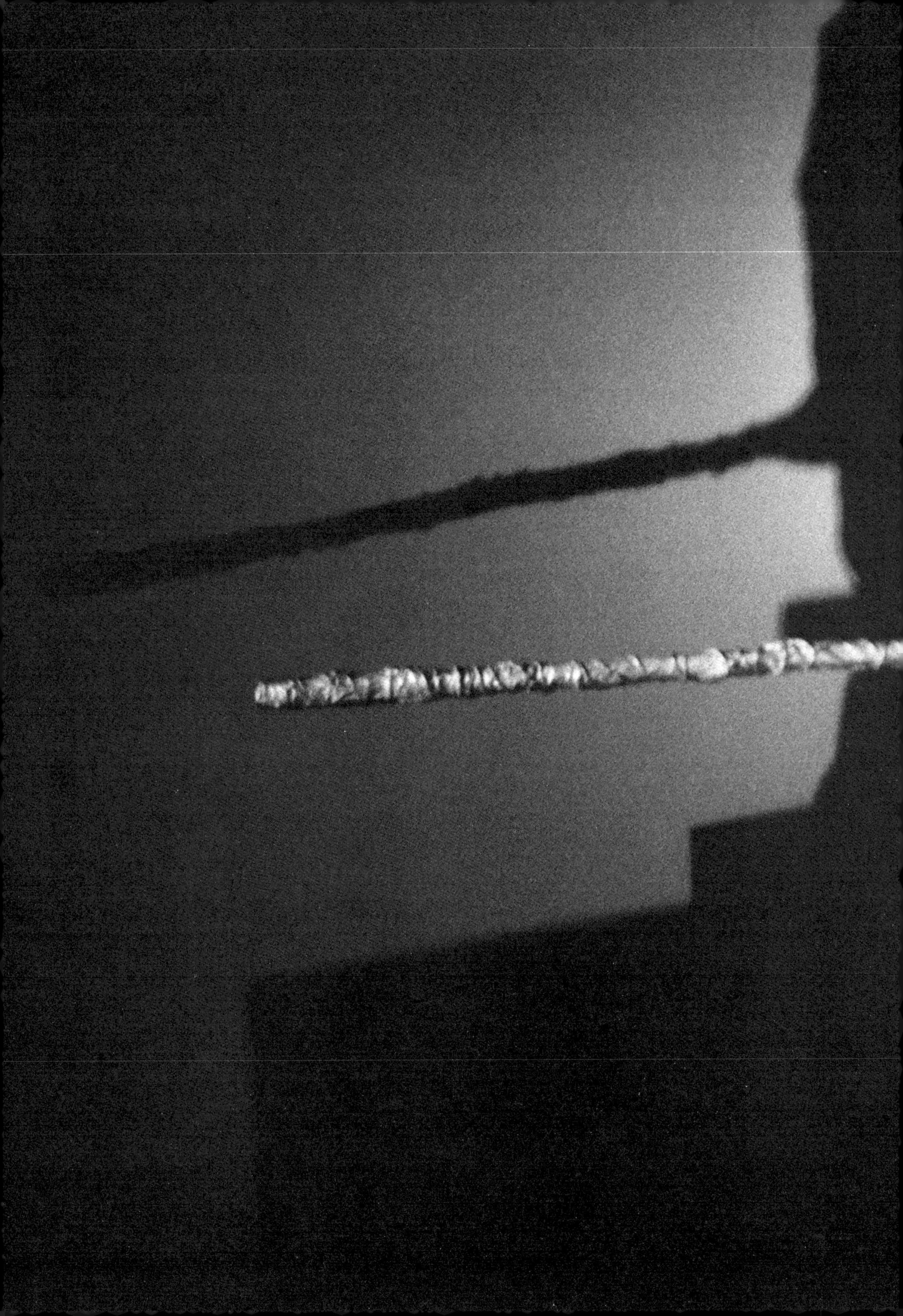

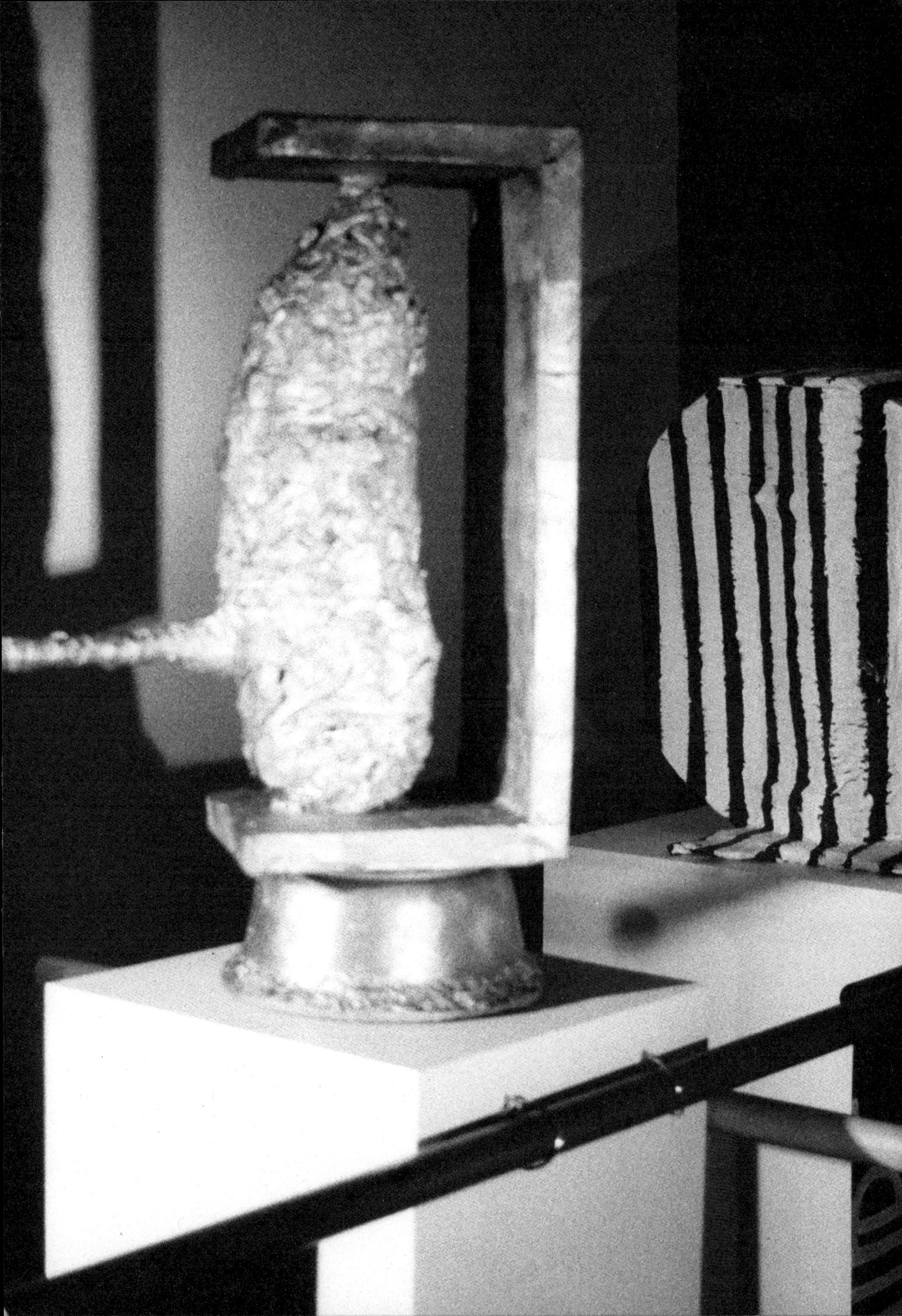

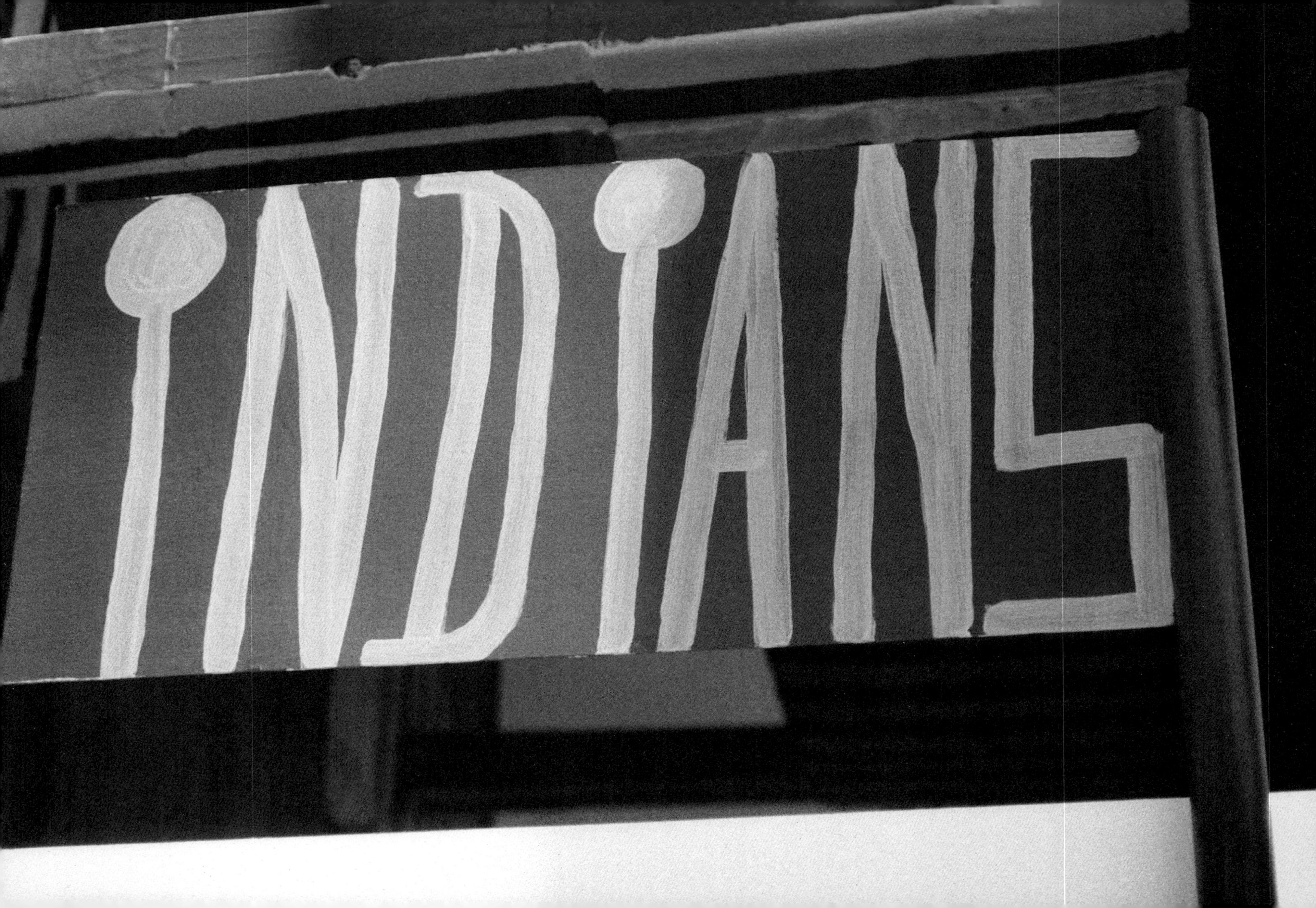
INDIANS

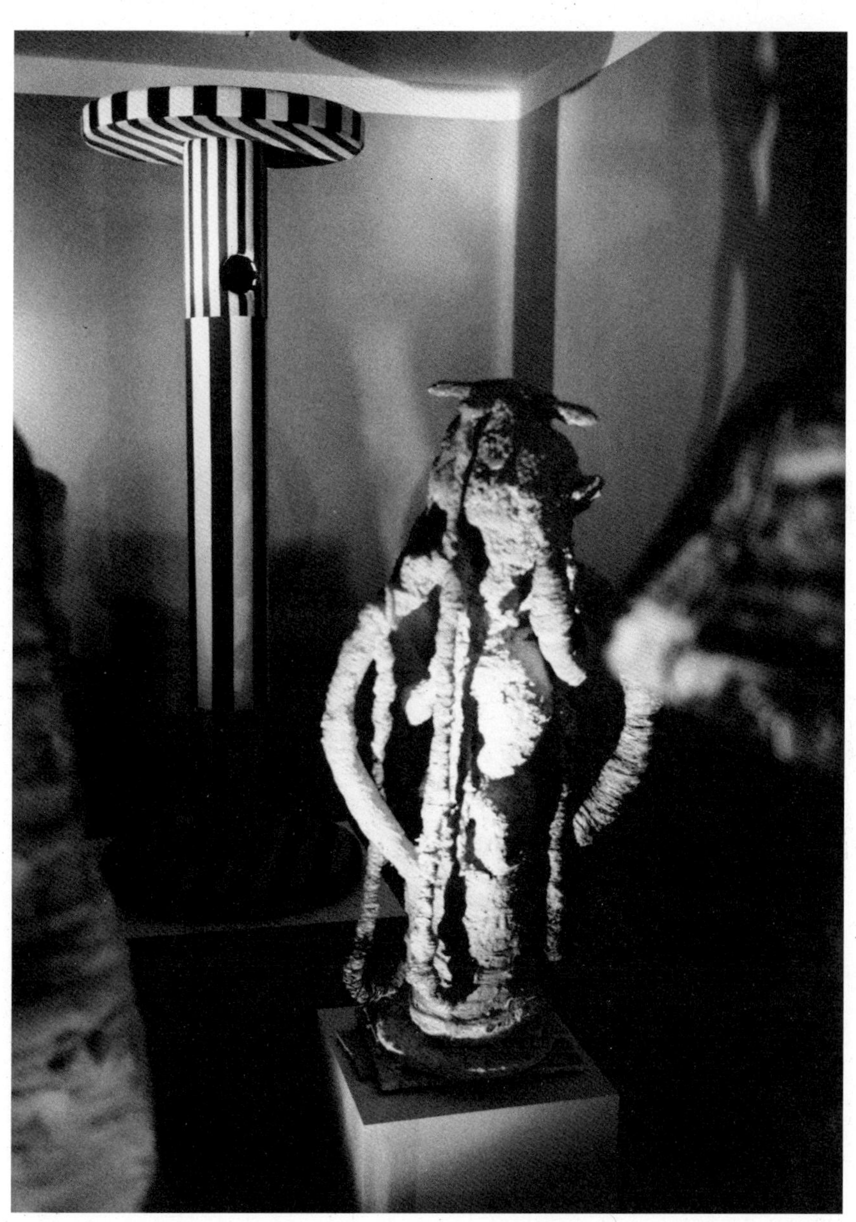

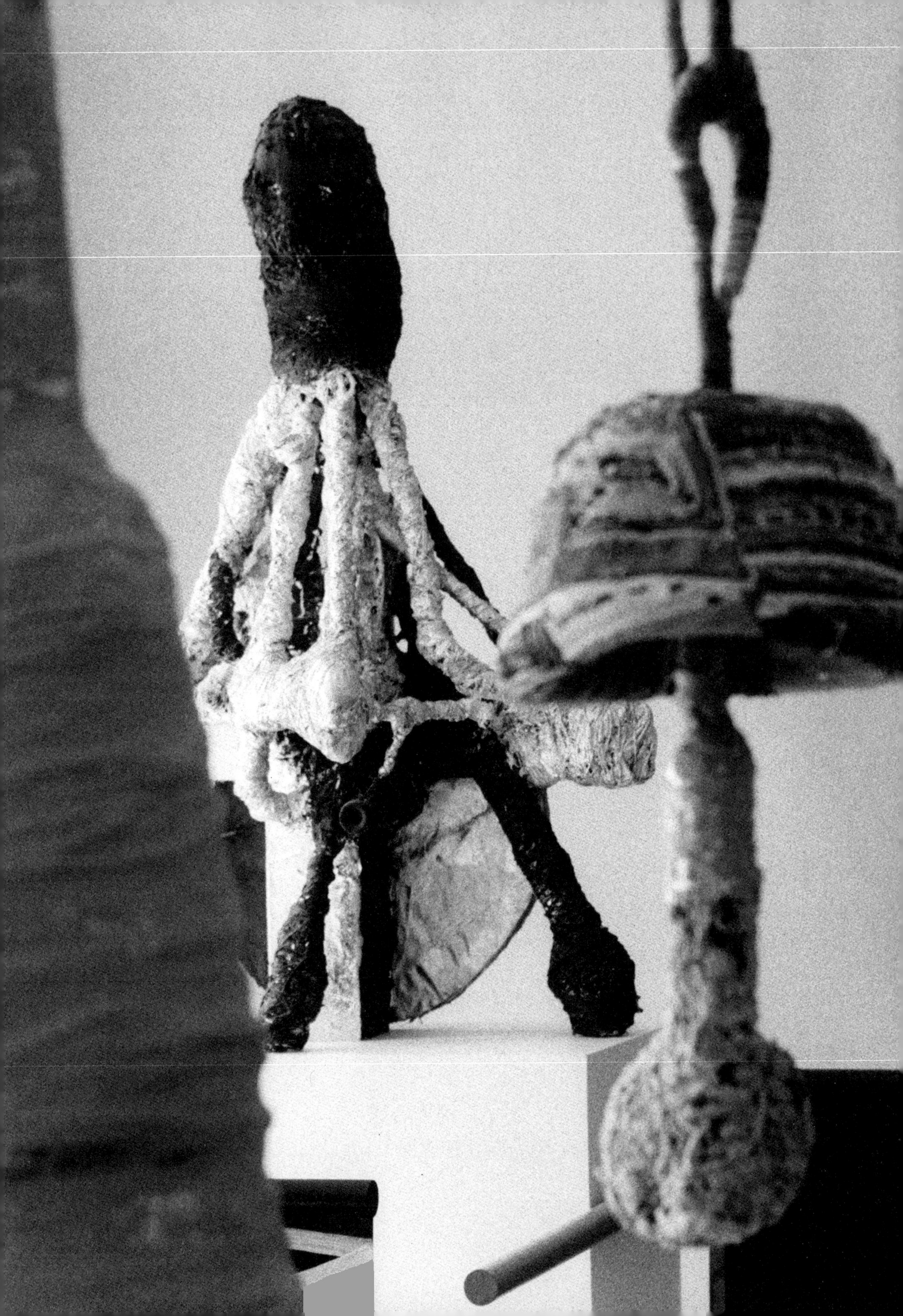

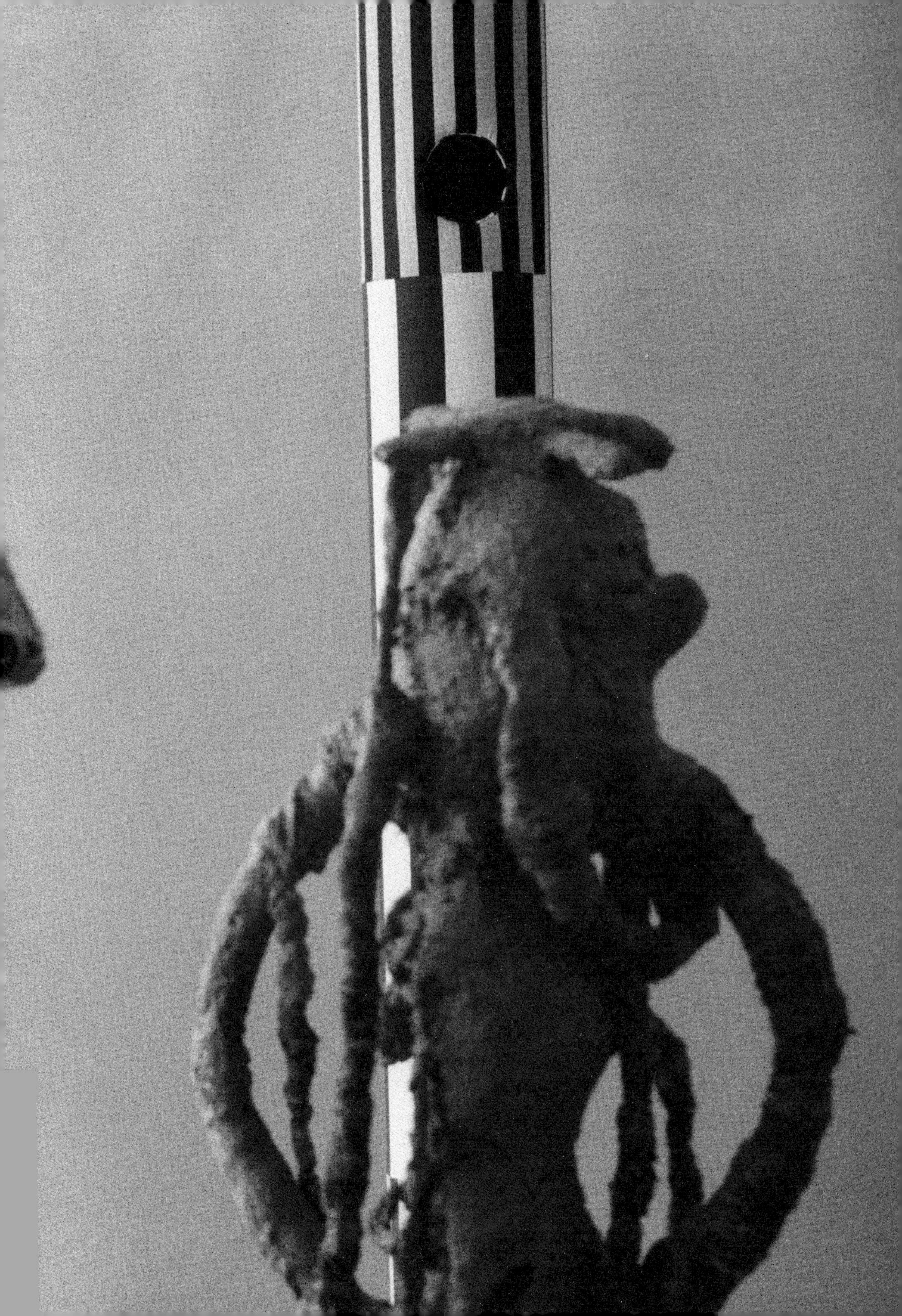

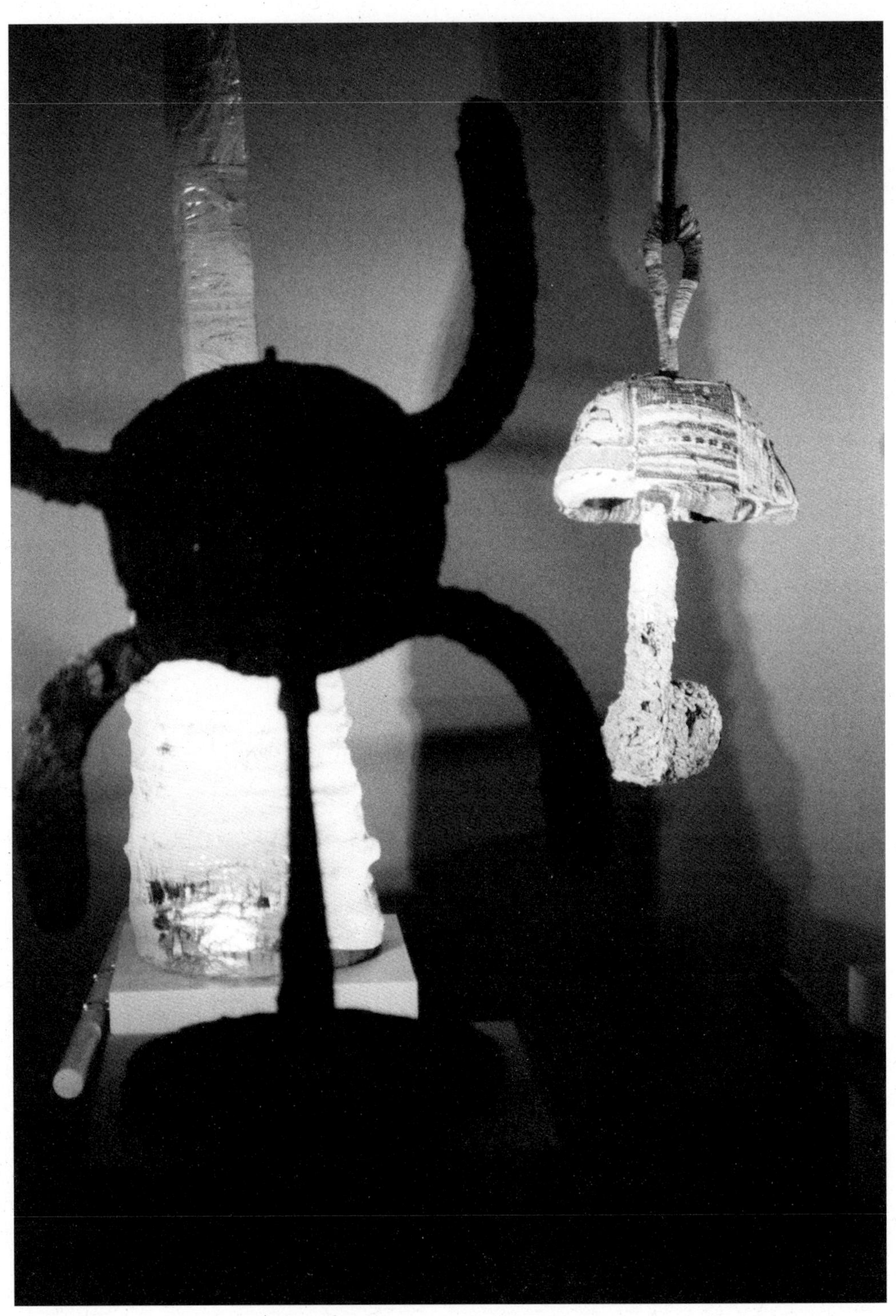

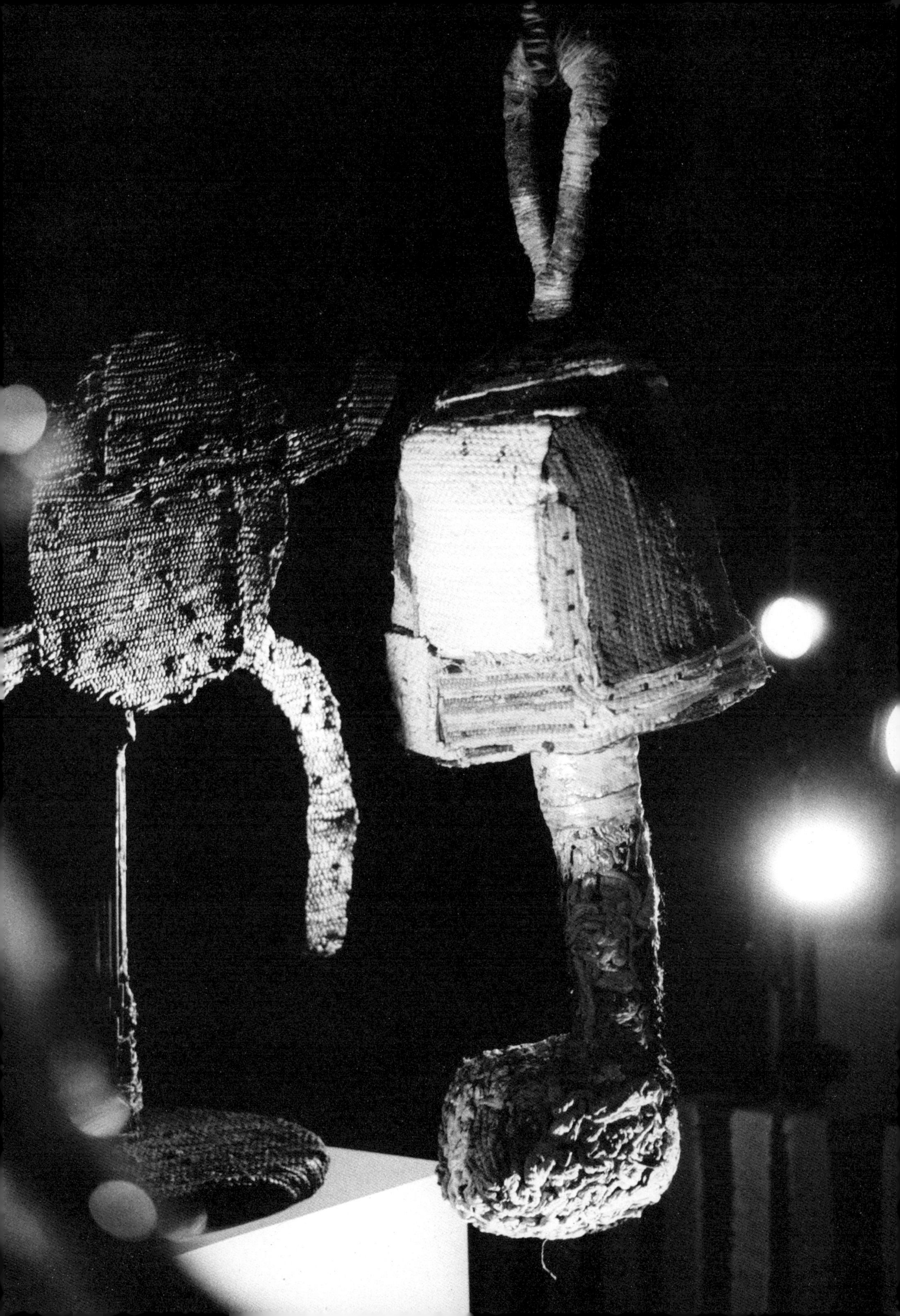

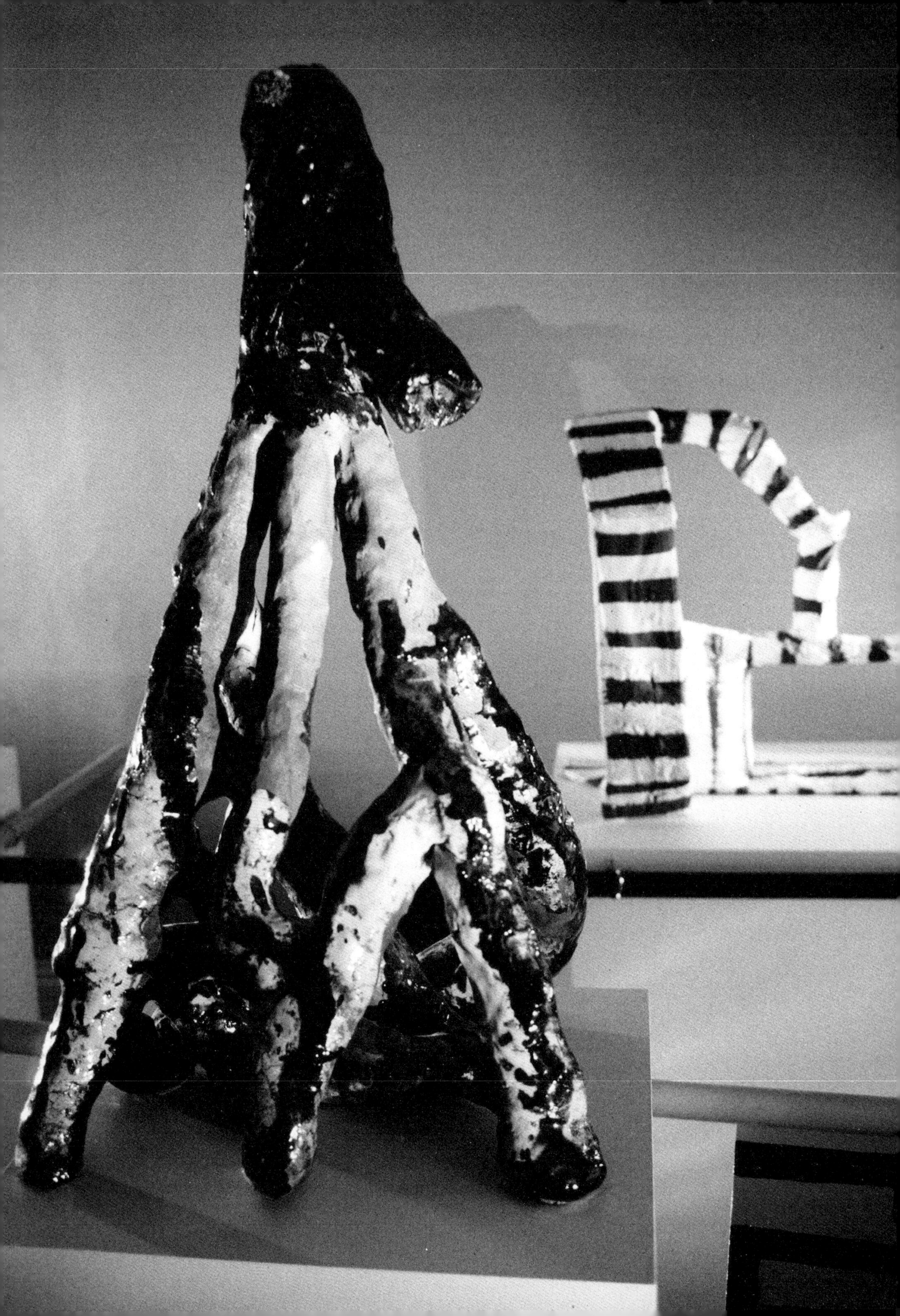

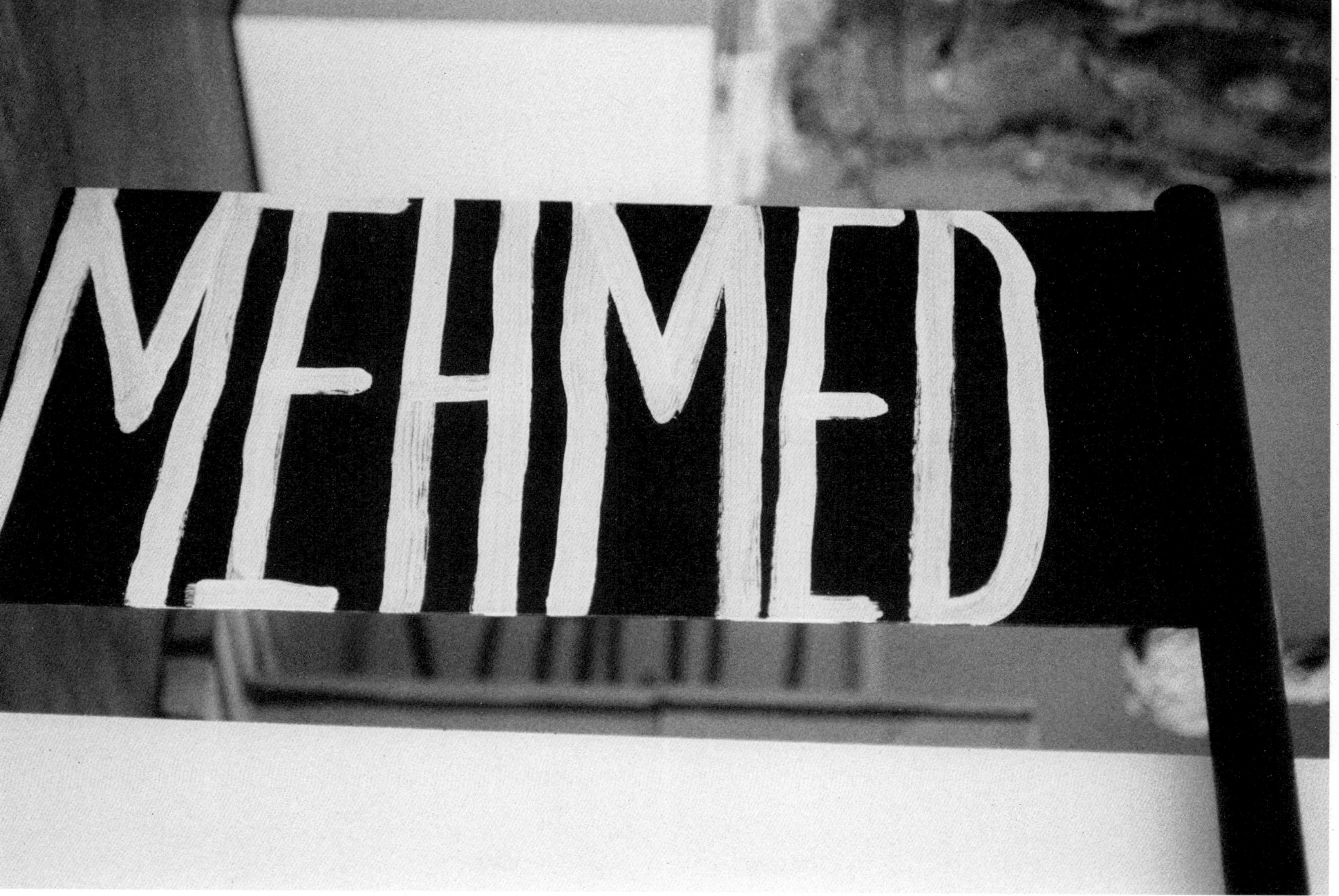
MEHMED

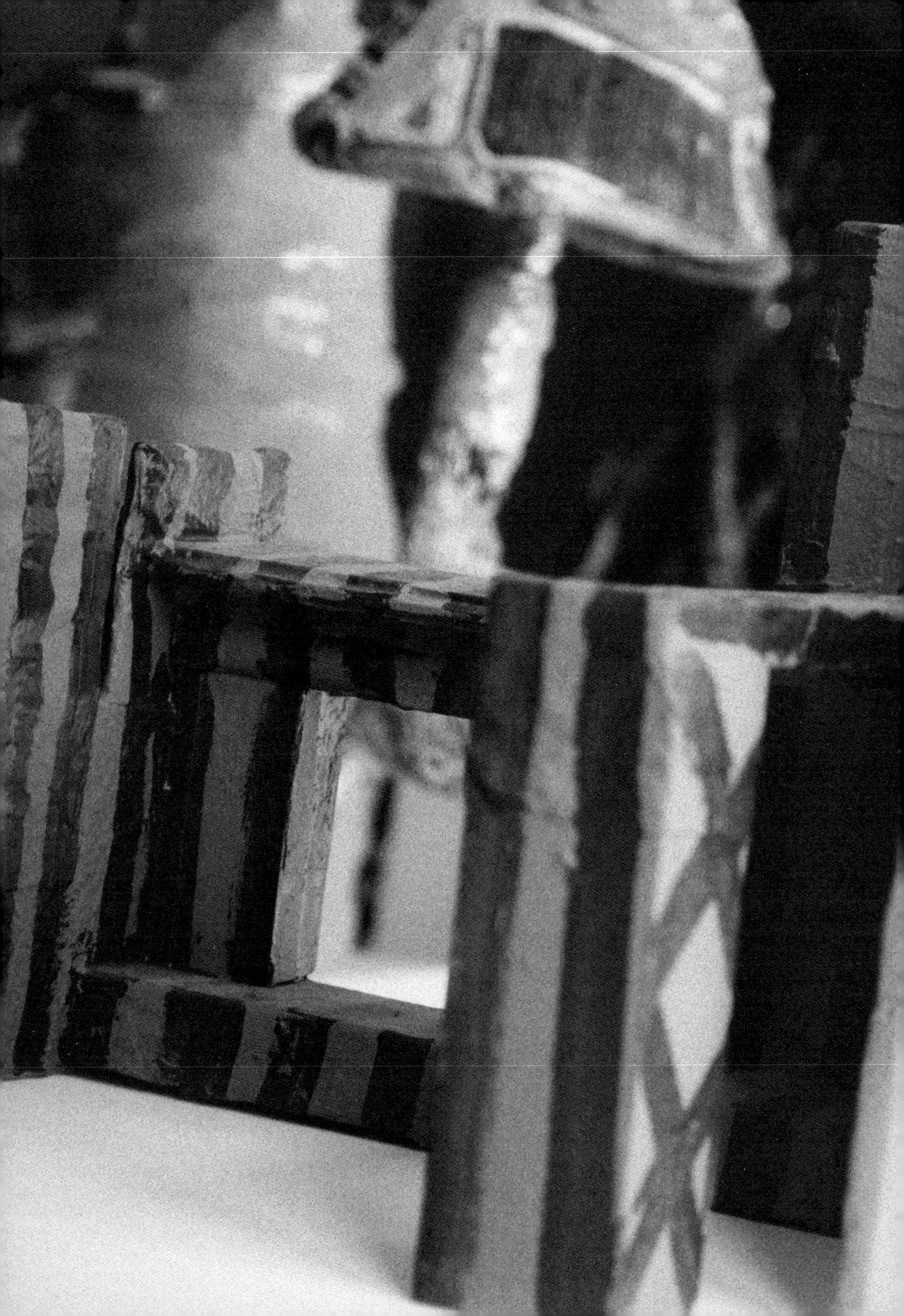

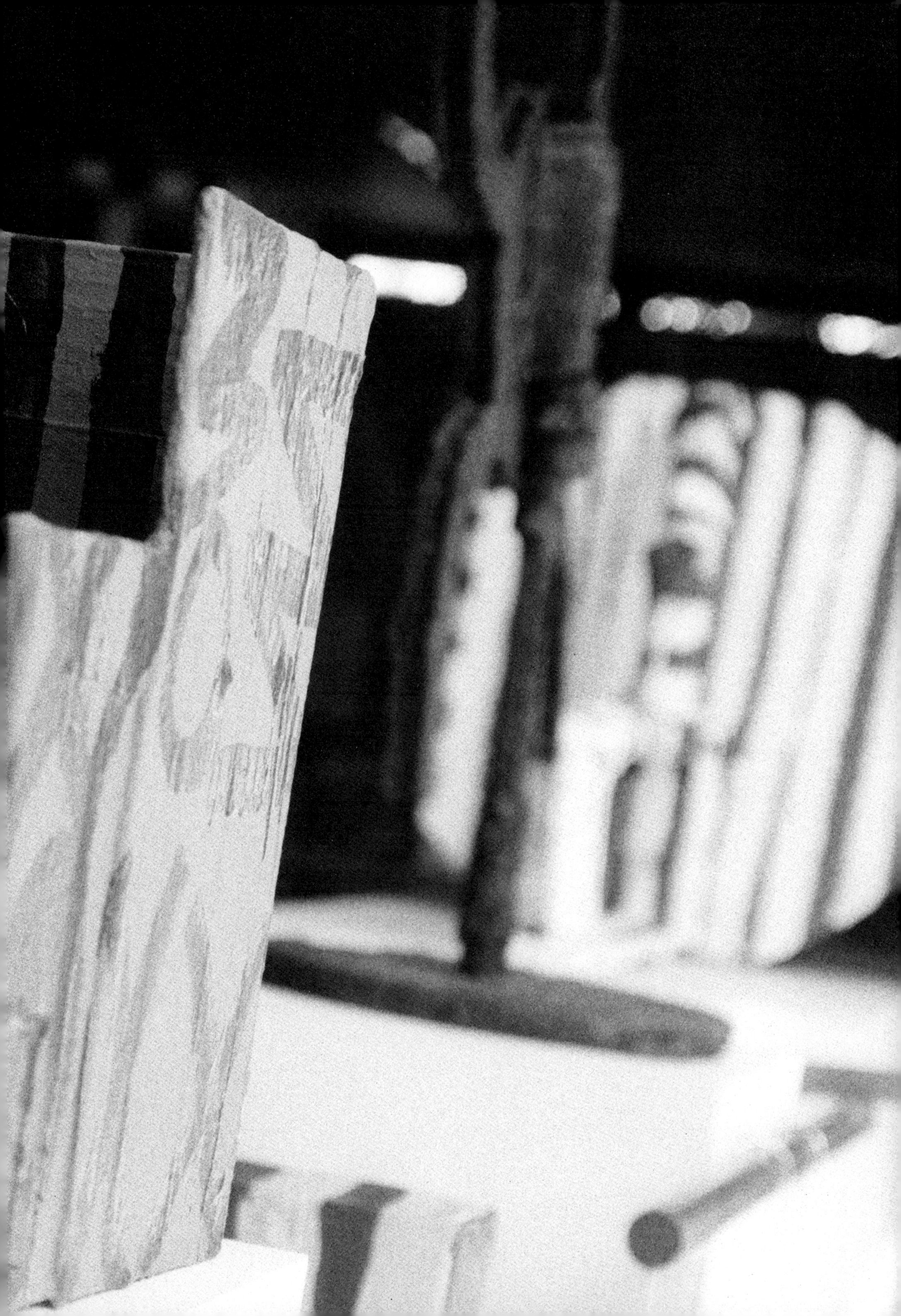

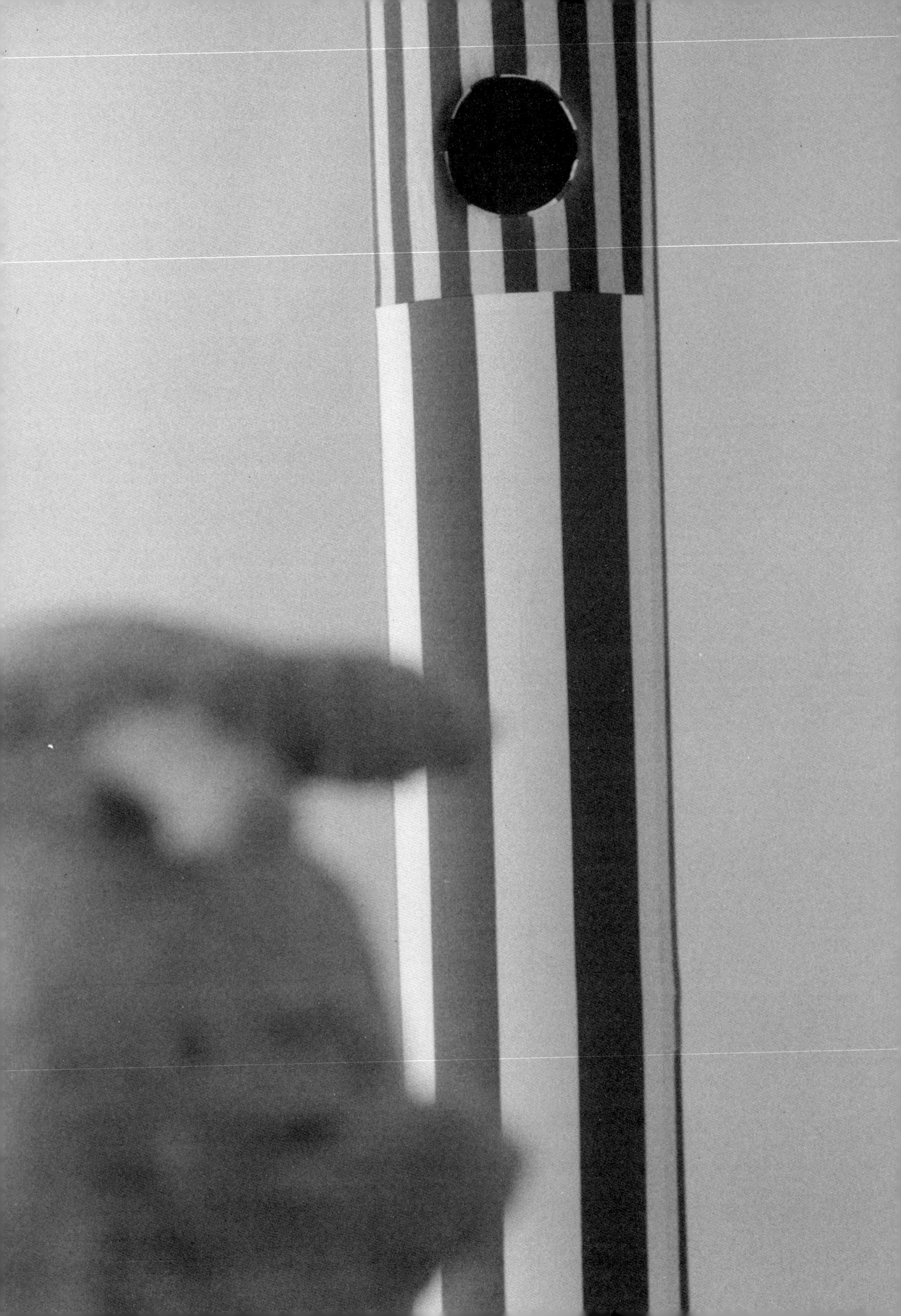

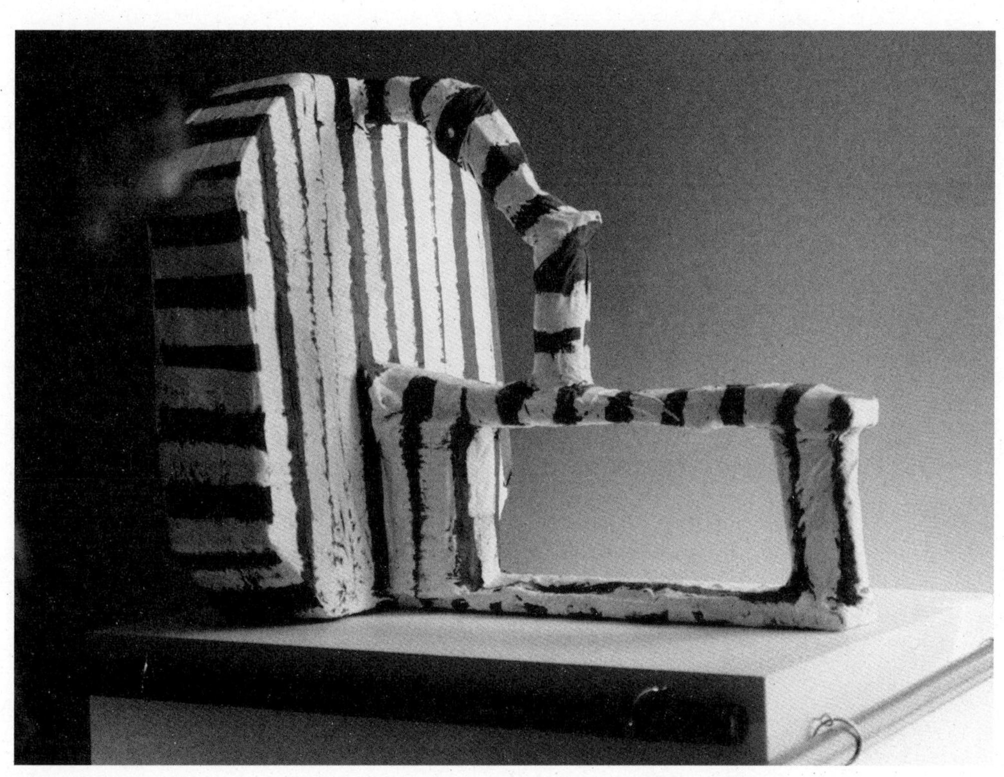

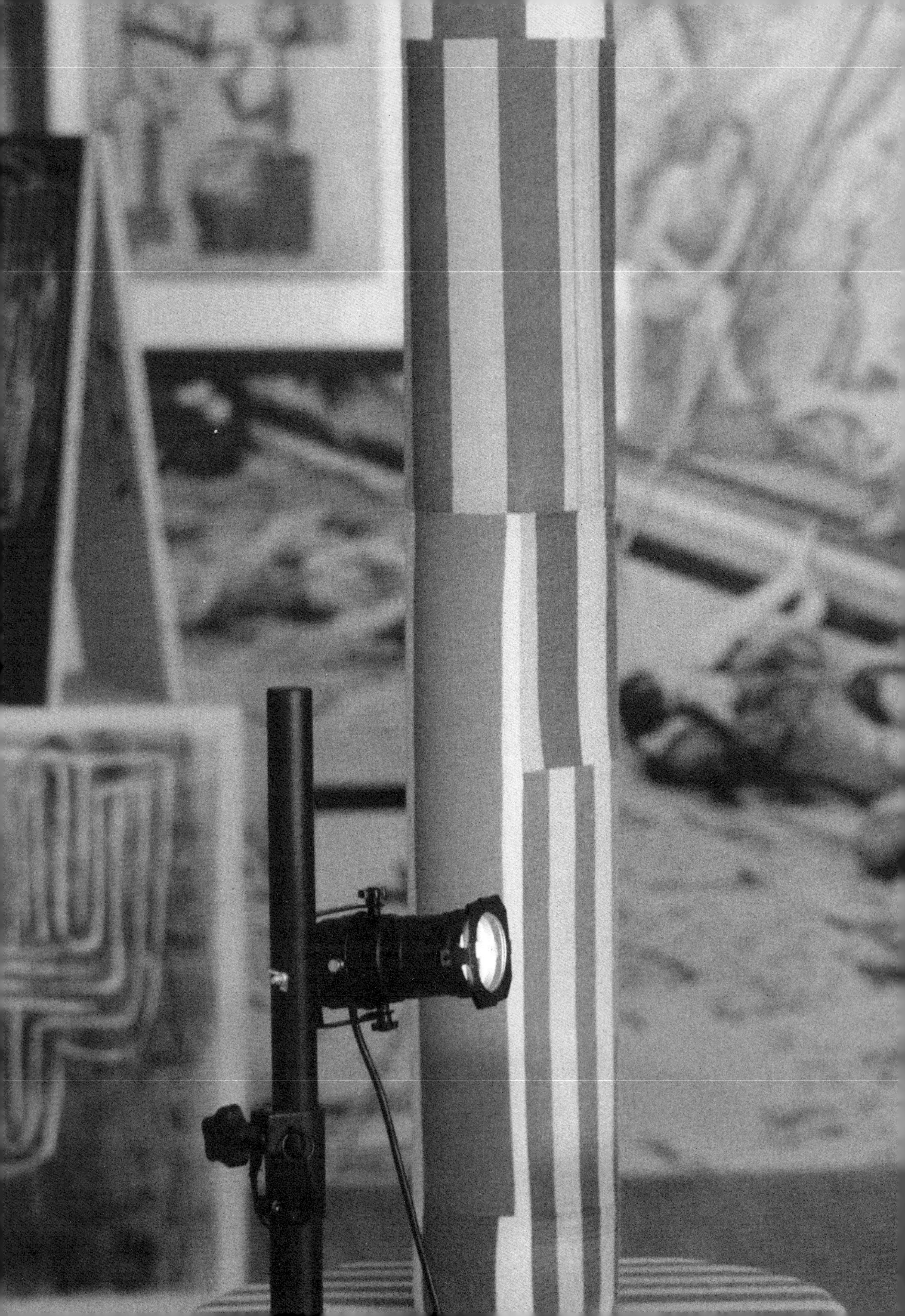

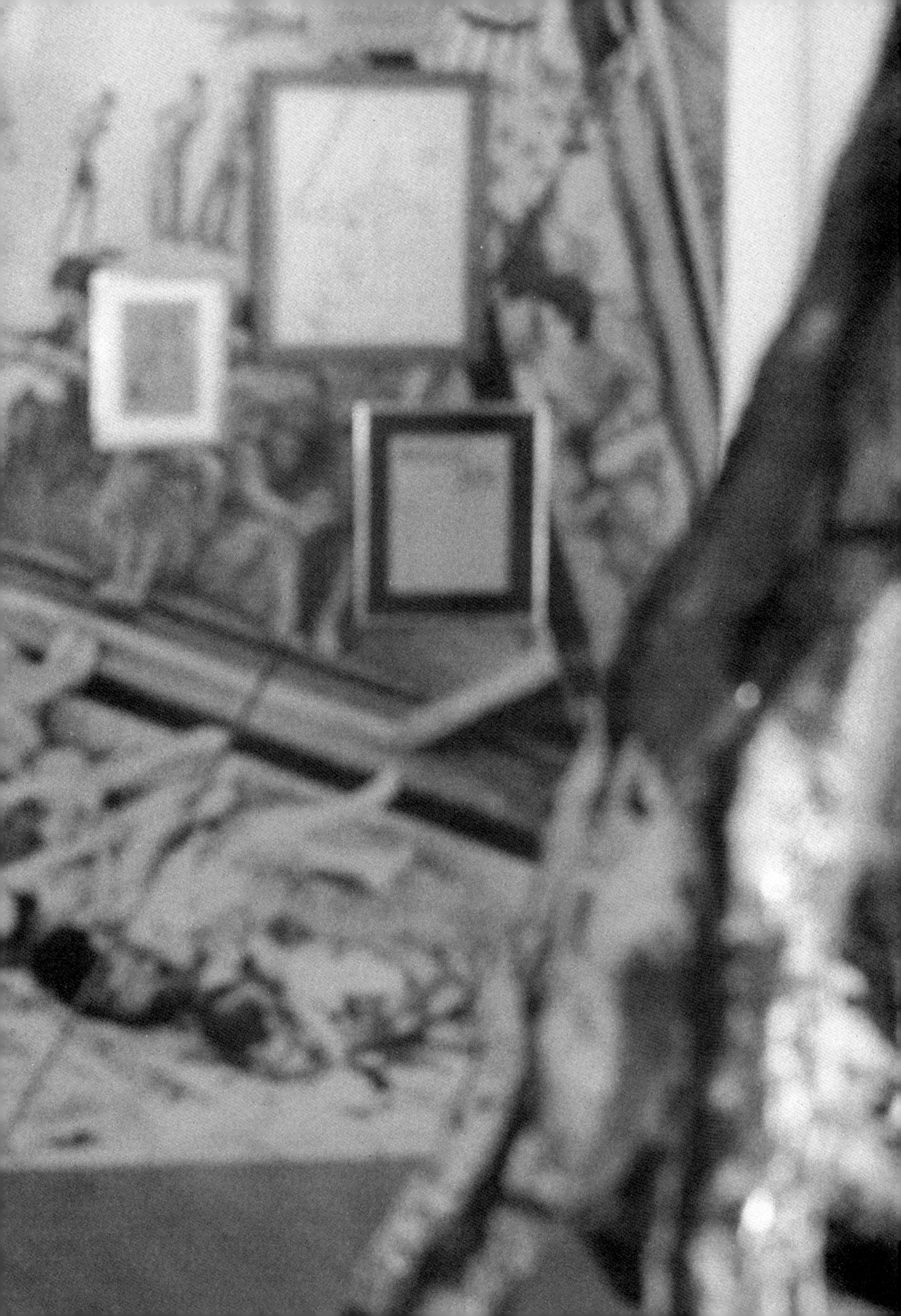

nürnberg
Flamenco Flametti
februar 4
2016

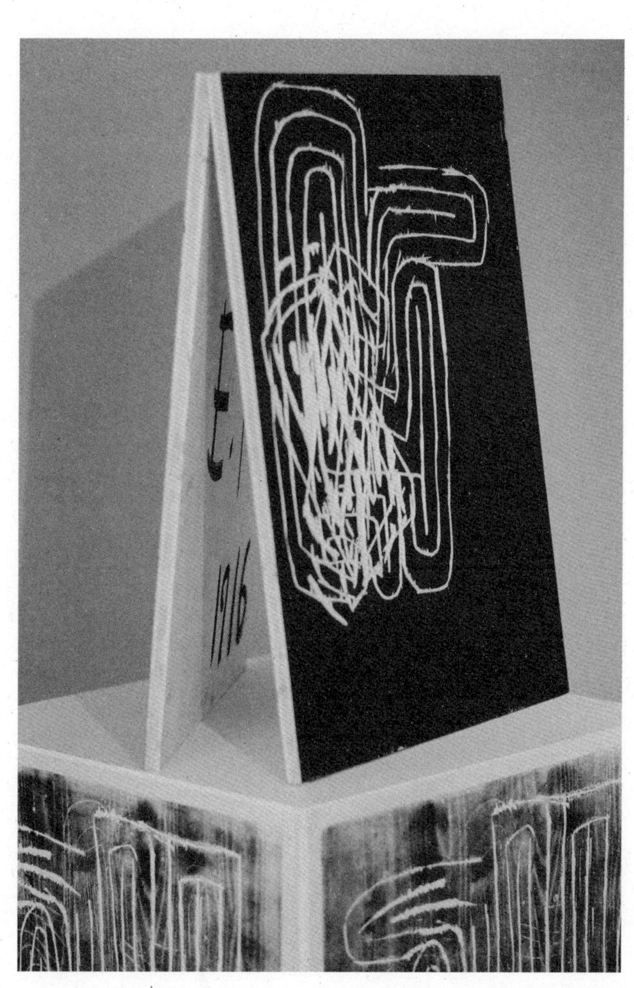

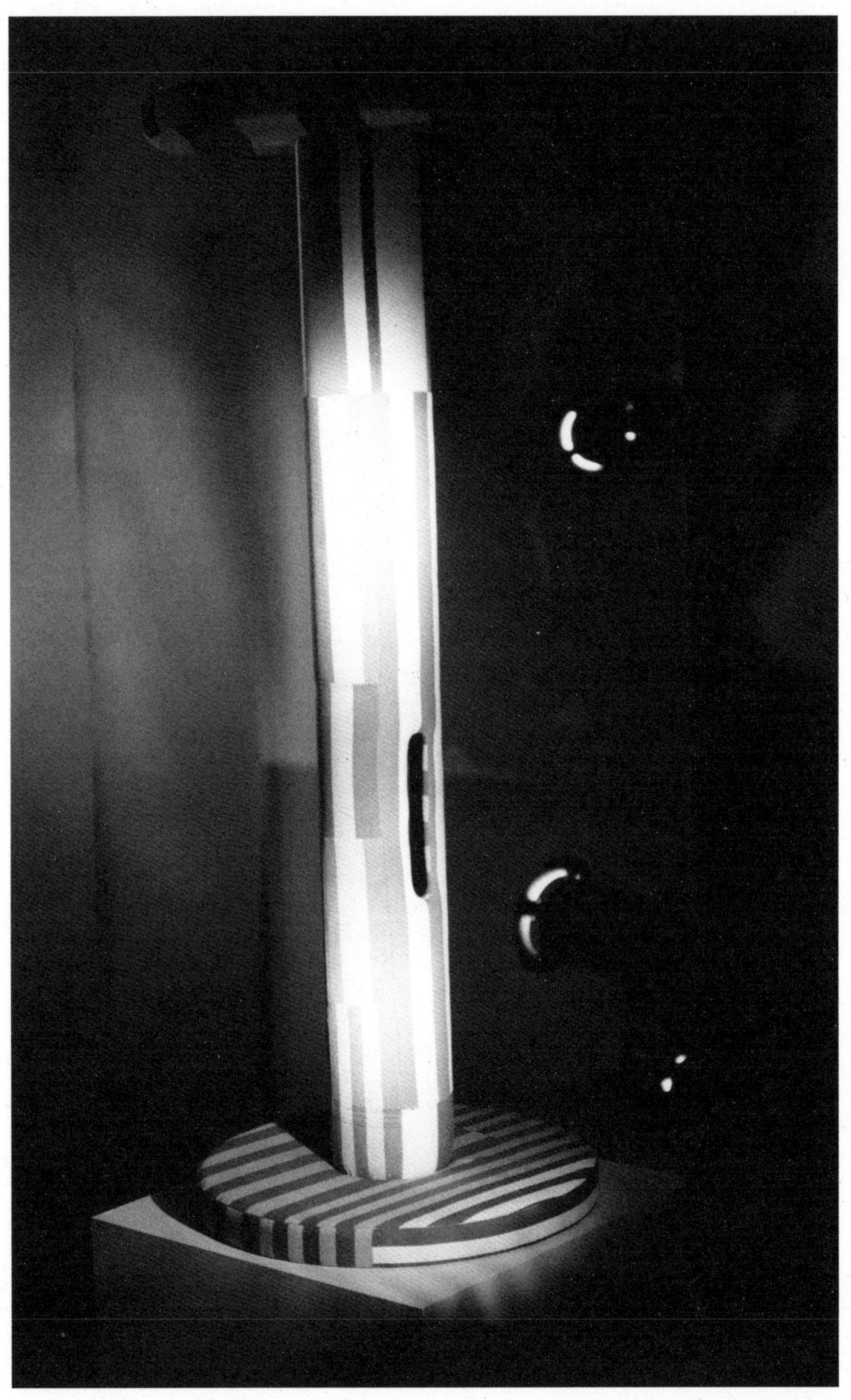

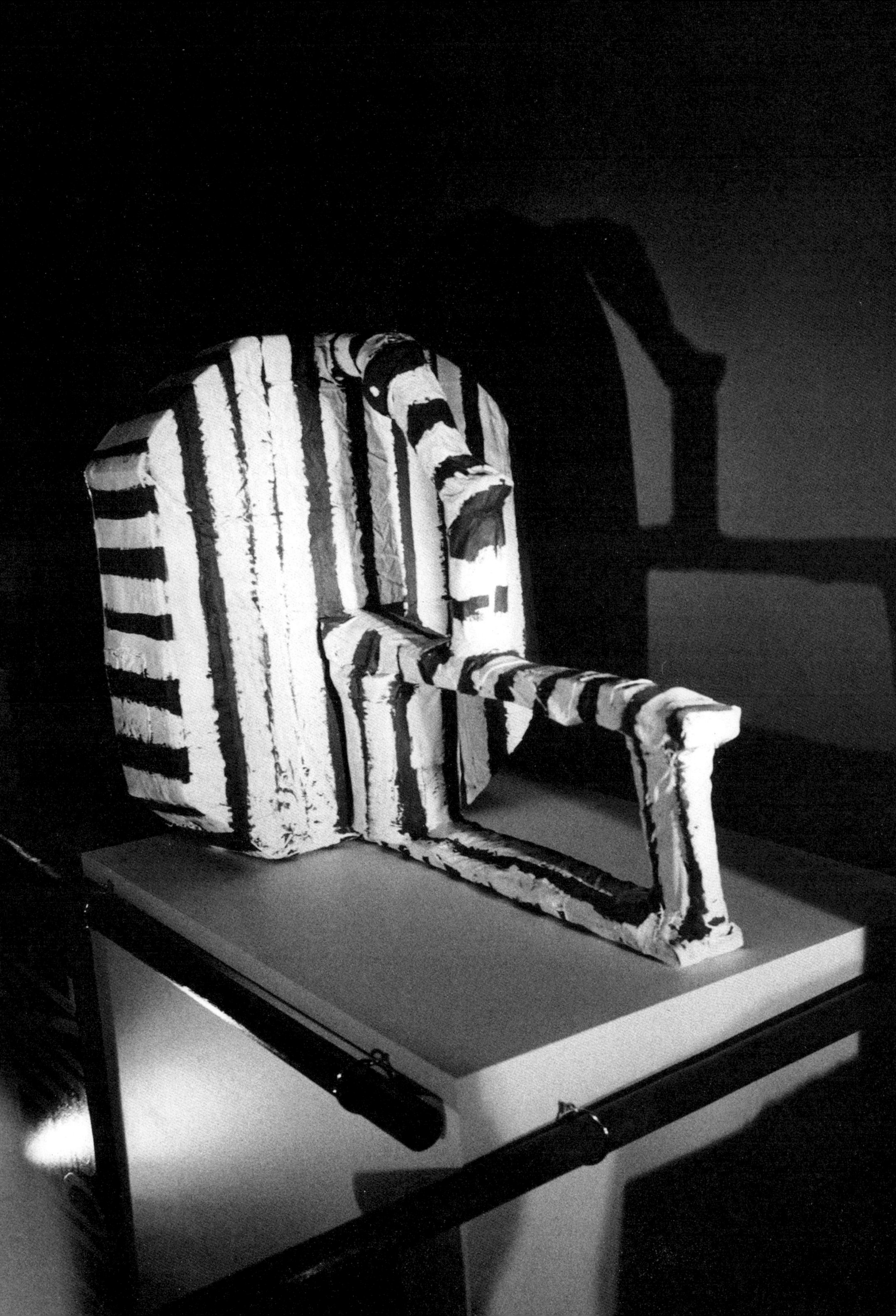

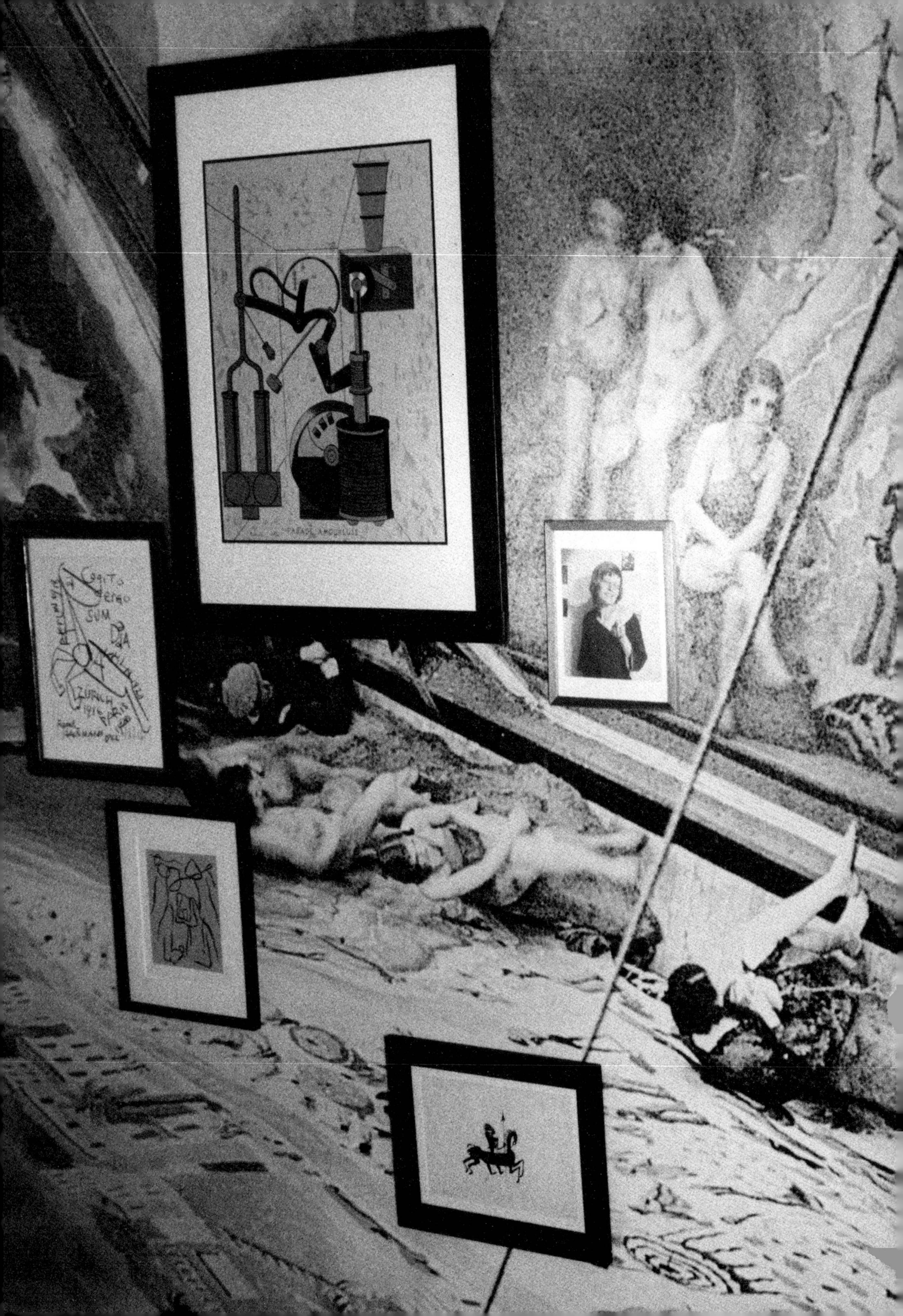

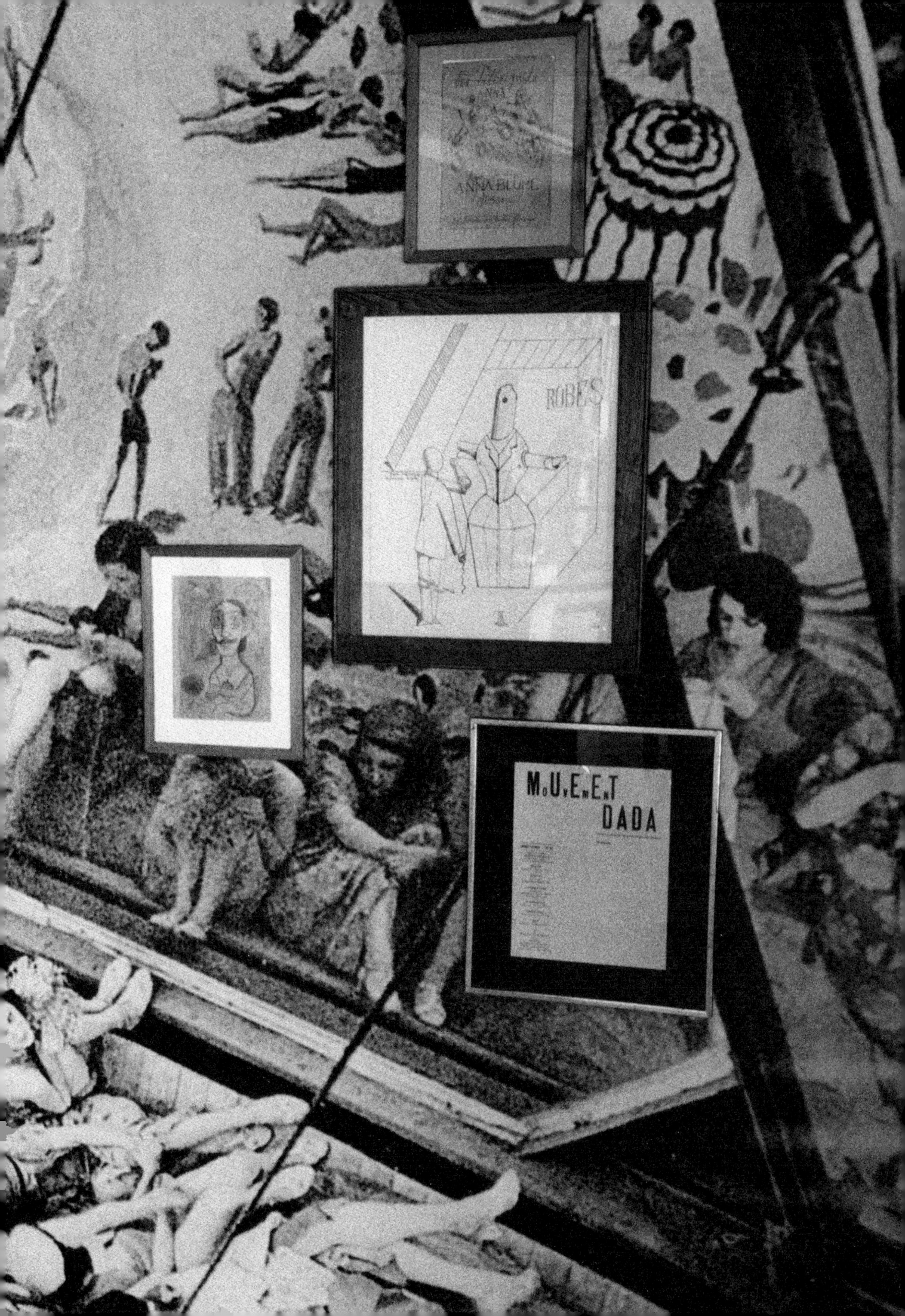
ROBES
MOUVEMENT DADA
ANNA BLUME

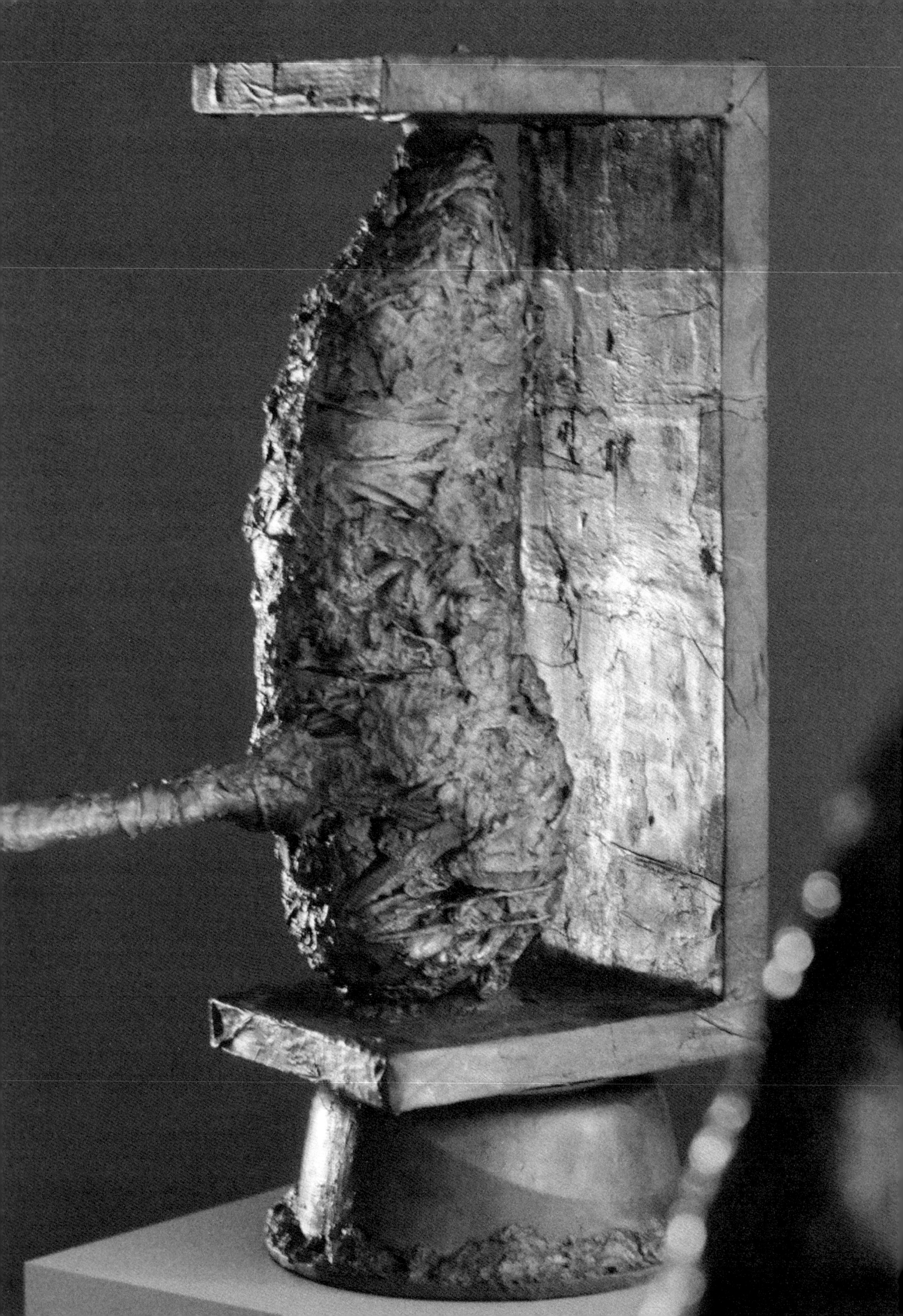

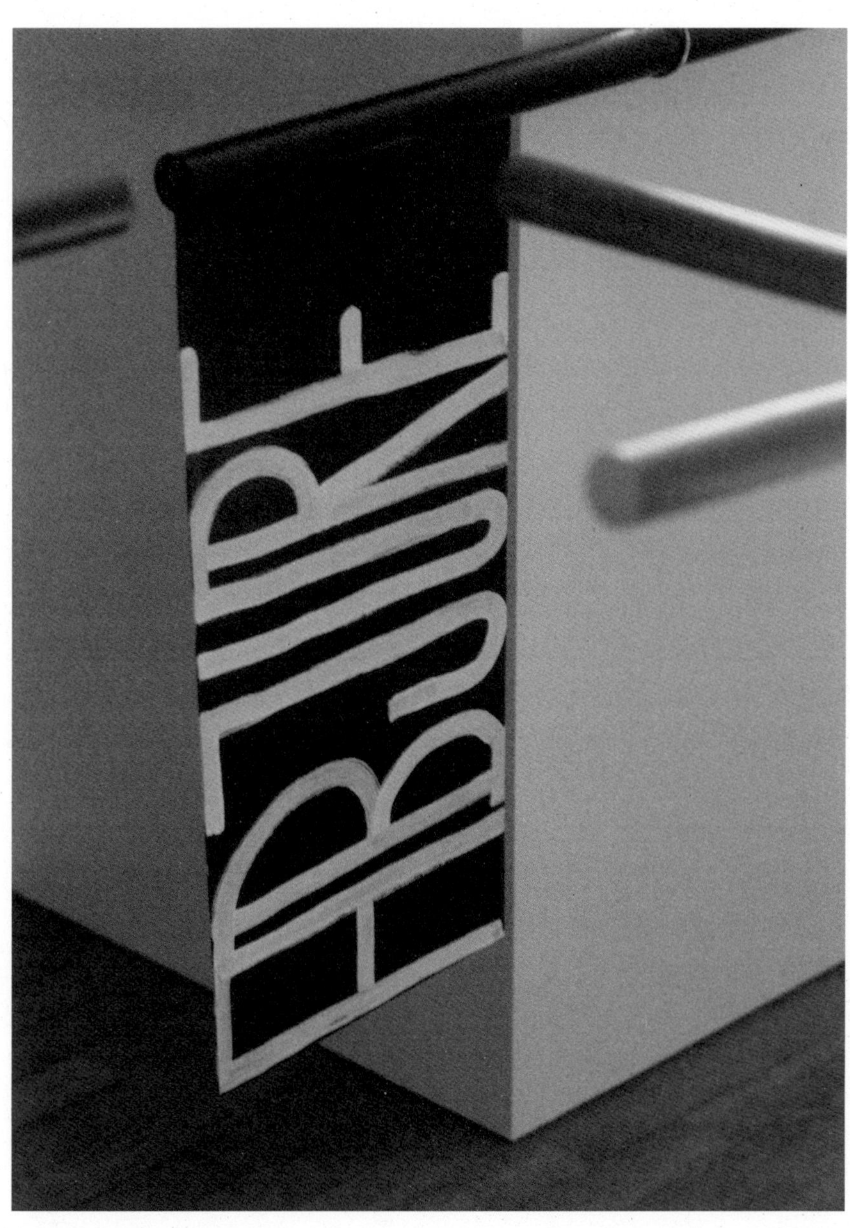
TRIBUNE

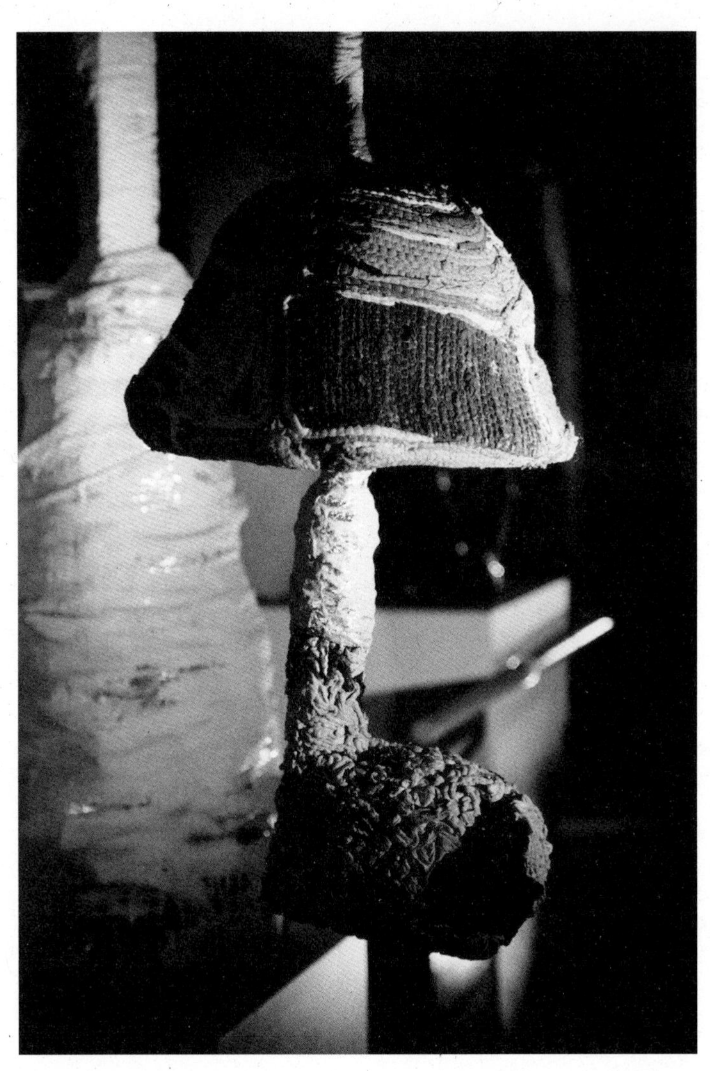

AUFRÄUMARBEITEN

Es war schon Hochsommer im Jahr 1958, als der Kunstverein für die Rheinlande und Westfalen in Düsseldorf mit der Ausstellung *DADA* die ersten institutionellen Aufräum-arbeiten zu einer inzwischen 40 Jahre in der Ferne liegenden Legende in Europa unter-nahm. Das Museum als Aktion getarnt versuchte unter Vermeidung von Experimenten, die Splitter einer Bewegung zu bergen und sie so zusammenzustückeln, dass aus dem zu-fällig Vereinzelten ein nach den Gesetzen des Zufalls geordnetes Ganzes werden konnte – ein Glück verheißendes Unterfangen. Die Handlungsform war nicht „kombinieren", son-dern „kitten". Es ging nicht um Collage, sondern um Kitt. Die Stichworte der Rekonst-ruktion waren im Jargon der Zeit schnell zur Hand: „wuchernder Wildtrieb am Wachs-tum der modernen Kunst", „schaubudenhafte Verzerrung", „reklamesüchtiger Klamauk", „Demonstration kindischer Albernheit" oder gleich in der Totale „fragwürdiger Unfug".

Die bahnbrechende MoMA-Ausstellung, die als erste mit der Genealogie *Fantastic Art, Dada and Surrealism* noch 1936 den großen Bogen gespannt hatte, und erst recht Robert Motherwells in Künstlerateliers gefeierte Monografie *The Dada Painters and Poets* hatten in der Wirtschaftswunderrepublik nur zwei Handvoll Menschen in Erinnerung – Initiierte eines kleinen Kreises von „Beteiligten". Alles andere war zunächst Propaganda von der falschen Seite, die einer anderen Kunst mit noch einmal anderen Kriterien voller Unverständnis gegenüberstand. Es war eine kleine Gruppe, die an DADA nicht nur erin-nern, sondern mit DADA eine „andere Tradition" in die heraufdämmernden Sixties zau-bern wollte und konnte.

DADA als Erfolg seiner Rezeptionsgeschichte in Europa beginnt hier.

DIE YOUNG STAY PRETTY

Viele der Dadas der ersten Stunde waren noch am Leben, und dass man sie im Dunst der Adenauerära immerhin als Überlebende der Moderne ansprechen konnte, hatte weni-ger mit ihren Werken als mit ihren oft von nomadischem Unterwegssein und grenzenloser Zerrissenheit bestimmten Biografien zu tun. Arp, Man Ray, Ribemont-Dessaignes, Max Ernst, Hannah Höch, Huelsenbeck, Tzara, Hausmann, Hans Richter und Duchamp leben noch. Schwitters, Picabia, Ball, Emmy Hennings und Sophie Taeuber sind längst zurück zu den Sternen. Auch wenn die Künstlerinnen und Künstler in dieser Ausstellung nur als Schatten auftreten, alle ihre von vorneherein einkalkulierten Einwände und Widersprüche und ihre „Kolumbus hat nicht Amerika entdeckt"-Attitude lässt DADA '58 als „Haltung" ins offene Meer auslaufen, als Schiff getarnt, ein Floß. Man rettet sich, um das Phänomen zu beschreiben, über die bekannten Inseln, von DADA Zürich über DADA New York, von DADA Paris nach DADA Berlin. Und im Akt der Verzweiflung greift man schweren Herzens zur Vokabel der „Bewegung". Das lassen die Künstler durchgehen, sie sind älter geworden, und sie alle sind froh, noch einmal die beste Geschichte ihrer Jugend zu erzählen. Aus Limoges schreibt Hausmann lakonisch: „Diese Bewegung hat wichtige Beiträge zur Psychologie des Individuums und der Massen sowie des bildenden Künstlers und des Dichters geliefert." Max Ernst ist da schon verhalten ungehalten, wenn er, während einer Partie Boule im ebenfalls ländlichen Huismes, gegenüber Patrick Waldberg, einem alten Spielgefährten, äußert: „Ich weiß, ich weiß, eine DADA-Ausstellung. Noch eine! Was haben nur all diese Leute, dass sie aus DADA ein Museumsstück machen wollen?" Und Klartext weiter: „DADA war eine Bombe." Und zum Schluss: „Es ist der Vorzug von DADA – jung gestorben zu sein."

K. O. IN DER VIERTEN RUNDE

Flamingo Fernande wurde auch nicht müde, von ihrer großen Zeit zu erzählen, den Jahren auf dem kleinen Hügel über Paris, der Butte Montmartre, kurz nach der Jahrhundertwende und noch vor dem Großen Krieg. Beiläufig süffisant die Geschichte, dass Flamingo Pablo mächtig stolz darauf war, dass man ihn und seine Entourage, die *bande à Picasso*, alles unbekannte Dichter und glücklose Maler, in manchen Teilen des Viertels recht ziellos umherschweifend, durchaus für eine Gang von Boxern hielt. Das war besser als Künstler – zumindest potenziell gefährlich. Flamingo Cravan blieb es freilich vorbehalten, den Spagat des Dichters als Boxer zu professionalisieren, wenn auch alle wussten, dass Flamingo Gauguin, wenn es darauf ankam, ebenso schnell bei der Sache gewesen war und Flamingo Braque bis ins hohe Alter seine gefürchteten linken Haken trainierte. Cravan verlor in Barcelona gegen den Schwergewichtsweltmeister *el gran* Jack Johnson, und der Kampf war echt. K.o. in der sechsten Runde – das bezahlte die Schiffspassage nach New York.

In ihrem anti-ideologischen Kampf gegen die Tradition und für eine „andere Moderne" waren die Flamingos alsbald auf merkwürdige Probleme gestoßen. Wie könnte die dumme Unterscheidung zwischen glücklichem Spiel und Verantwortungsbewusstsein und wie erst das Dilemma einer radikalen Kritik an der „Weltzerstörung" bei gleichzeitigem Festhalten an einem romantisch gefärbten Ideal in Balance gebracht werden? Wie die als „Form und Prozess" betrachtete, „gelungene und echte Kunst" einbetten in eine stets in Bewegung befindliche und permanent neu zu verhandelnde Aktion? Wo war das Ding, das im Ergebnis „keine Kunst" war und trotzdem als Kick durchgehen konnte, der einem das Leben erträglich machte, zumindest so weit, dass ein Überleben überhaupt in Betracht kam. War es schon zu viel verlangt, die „Poesie des Alltagslebens" als die eigentliche Erscheinungsform der Kunst anzusehen und ihr Ergebnis, das hoch gelobte

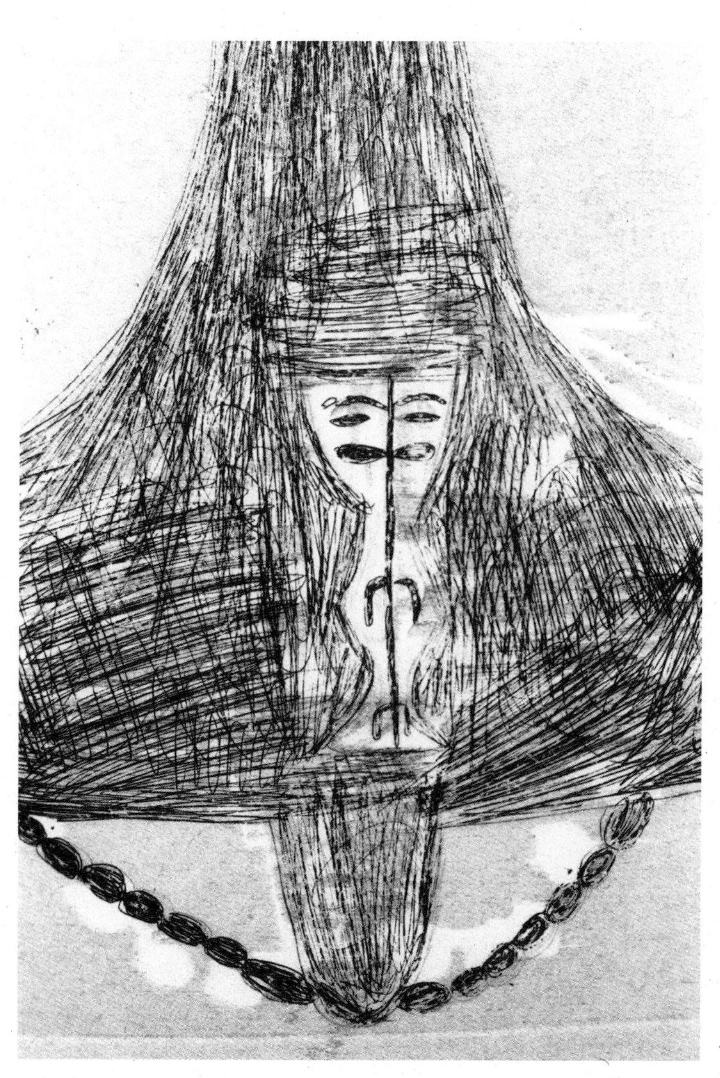

Kunstwerk des Einzelgenies, als längst überholtes Relikt, als Rest zu betrachten. War Schachspielen so gut wie Kunst? Ist jedes Aquarell größer als eine Hand schon Sport? Wo waren die Modelle, mit denen sich schnörkelfrei hantieren ließ, und wo war ein Publikum, das wenigstens bereit war, diese Unterkante der ermüdeten Zivilisation abzustützen?

Ein paar Groschen Eintritt in die Zirkuswelt, die mussten doch zu finden sein. Das Bühnenrequisit, das nur dann in Erscheinung tritt, wenn „es" gespielt wird, und im Danach des Abends im Dazwischen der Vorstellung nichts anderes sein muss als ein abgelegtes Werkzeug, ein „Artefakt" für etwas, und das darüber hinaus von verschiedenen Akteuren unterschiedlich in Aktion gebracht werden kann. Das schien ein Ausweg, und Flamingo Franz West wird ein solches 60 Jahre später ein „Passstück" nennen. Es ist die Idee des objet trouvé rückwärts, es ist das verlorene Objekt, das nach der Tournee verschwindet, unbestimmt auf dem Dachboden der Concierge landet oder nie mehr wieder entdeckt wird. Zunächst hilft dem Requisit ein „Sockel", und im Verlauf der Geschichte lernen wir, dass die Überseetransportkiste mit beiliegender Inventarliste das vorläufige Finale bedeutet. Flamingo Picabia findet im Reparaturbedarf das Modell für sein *Portrait d'une jeune fille americaine dans l'état de nudité* und Duchamp das Fahrrad-Rad. Heute wissen wir auch, dass *So ein Ding will ich auch haben* und *Fill with own imagination* über schwierige Zeiten hinweghelfen ...

DAS FELL DES BÄREN

Rainer Maria Rilke sitzt 1915 in der Münchner Wohnung der vermögenden Sammlerin Herta Koenig einem Bild gegenüber, das diese sich vor Kurzem beim Avantgarde-Galeristen Thannhauser gesichert hatte, der es wiederum am Vorabend des Ersten Weltkriegs bei der Versteigerung eines Kunstfonds, der sich metaphorisch hochgerechnet *Das Fell des Bären* nannte, in Paris erworben hatte. Es war schon der Größe nach der bisher bedeutendste verkaufte Picasso, und der auf der öffentlichen Versteigerung erzielte Preis hatte nicht nur den Investoren fabelhaften Gewinn, den Kritikern ein ernstzunehmendes Thema, sondern vor allem auch dem Künstler Aufmerksamkeit, Ruhm und sogar Gewinnbeteiligung beschert. Flamingo Picasso hatte im Sommer 1905 mit großem Tam-Tam begonnen, sein programmatisches Bild zu entwickeln, und „die Familie der Seiltänzer", kurz *Les Saltimbanques* genannt, war von Anbeginn an als „mehr" gedacht als die Schilderung einer Artistenfamilie backstage. In Rilkes 5. Duineser Elegie dann die pathosseligen Zeilen:

„WER aber *sind* sie, sag mir, die Fahrenden, diese ein wenig
Flüchtigern noch als wir selbst, die dringend von früh an
wringt ein *wem, wem* zu Liebe
niemals zufriedener Wille?"

Die im Zeilenfall folgende Schilderung der Akrobaten – „der alte, der nur noch trommelt", und „der junge, der Mann, als wär er der Sohn eines Nackens und einer Nonne", bis hin zur „selten zärtlichen Mutter" – atmet schwer, und die nächste Vorstellung ist die schwerste und das Winterquartier noch nicht einmal ausgemacht. Die vielbeschworene Faszination der Künstler am Zirkus, am Varieté wird so in das Klischee der Randexistenz in einer Gesellschaft gebettet, dass bis heute die Grenze unscharf bleibt, ob die Poesie, die Verfahrensweise oder die Metaphern die Form beschwören.

SLACKLINE

Giovanni Domenico war Tiepolos Sohn und mit seinem Bruder Lorenzo von Kindesbeinen an in die gigantischen Kunst-am-Bau-Projekte seines Vaters verstrickt. Dass *les deux frères* selbst Maler werden mussten, zeigt die Selbstverständlichkeit der profanen Weitergabe eines gut laufenden Familienbetriebs als Vererbung von Genie und Klasse. Als Legende spiegelt sie ein ebenso unausweichliches Schicksal wie die Geschichte vom Zirkuskind, das in den Sägespänen der Manege groß wird und so ohne Ausweg Seiltänzerin werden muss. Dass das Kind spindeldürr, aber muskulös ist, ist Segen und Fluch des abgetrotzten Daseins zugleich. Das vermeintliche Ideal von Schönheit kommt hier vom Hunger und mündet wieder in die gleiche Geschichte vom *peintre maudit*, der aus Verzweiflung jene zauberhaften Zeichnungen der Seiltänzerin mit einer Träne im Auge in den Ofen wirft, um nicht frieren zu müssen im Winter. Auf Flamingo Tiepolos Bild *Pulcinella e i saltimbanchi* liegen die Seile am Boden und tollkühn schlagen die Akrobaten Rad vor den staunenden Zuschauern; ohne Seil wäre das einfacher. Dem stilisierten Kostümrepertoire der Commedia dell'arte verdanken wir die weißen Kostüme der maskierten Clowns. Teil ihrer Erscheinung ist ein konischer Hut, der dem berühmtesten Foto der DADA-Zeit, Hugo Ball auf der Bühne des Cabaret Voltaire in Zürich 1916, verblüffend gleicht. Bei Flamingo Ball ist die improvisierte Papprolle mehr Harnisch als Kostüm und sogar als Kostüm mehr Kostümersatz. Dass Sophie Taeuber – um ihr Dasein als Lehrerin an der Kunstgewerbeschule nicht zu gefährden – stets nur „verkleidet" und mit Maske auf der Bühne erscheint und die gleichen Armstulpen mit den Fingerersatz-Papierhandschuhen auch auf einem der Fotos trägt, die sie in vollem Ornat mit Jancos Maske zeigen, lässt darüber hinaus auf einen vielfältigen und keiner Figur explizit zugeordneten Einsatz mancher Requisiten auf DADA-Bühnen schließen.

Erst die Rezeption macht Flamingo Ball aufgrund des Pressefotos unweigerlich zum King of DADA oder zumindest zu einem ungelenken Bischof. Weder König noch Bischof kann es im Sinne einer Verortung in einer Hierarchie im DADA-Kosmos geben, und Kosmos ist immer zu viel, und Kosmos ist billig, und nur die Widersprüchlichkeiten, die ein Pseudo-Chef-Foto über ein Jahrhundert entwickeln kann, bleiben interessant. Hugo

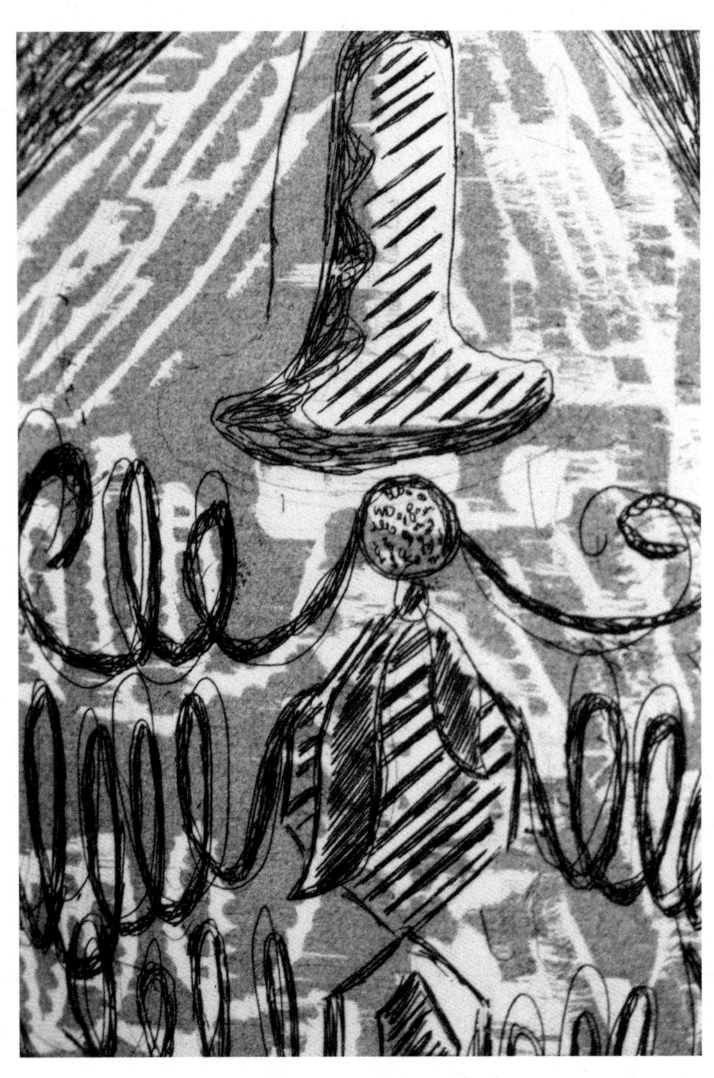

Ball steht als *the artist is present* mit eingefrorener Geste, Bewegung ausgeschlossen, am Anfang von DADA, und seine clevere Selbststilisierung atmet bereits Perfektion, als es weder einen richtigen Anfang noch das Wort DADA als Bezeichnung noch den Begriff DADA als Ausnahme von den vielgeplagten Ismen überhaupt gibt. Das Motiv gefällt dem Publikum zunehmend besser – es passt zum Label.

Am Anfang war das Wort Am – wird der Total-Flamingo Timm Ulrichs später titeln, ein sich selbst und sein Tun ernst nehmender Joker eines Spiels, in dem er, wenn nötig, sogar Anna Blume heiratet, die bekanntlich auch anderen Flamingos stets zugeneigt war und blieb. Emmy Hennings ist „Pretty Flamingo".

THE REAL FLAMETTI

Das Wort DADA kommt in Hugo Balls *Flametti oder Vom Dandysmus der Armen* selbstverständlich nicht vor. Es ist ein Roman, der wenig verschlüsselt, das Milieu und das eigensinnig organisierte, aber doch seltsam ziellose Dasein einer Varietétruppe zum Thema hat, dessen Anspielungen auf lebende Personen aber ansonsten als rein zufällig und selbstverständlich nicht beabsichtigter Teil des Plots verhandelt werden. Heute ist Flametti mit Sicherheit der Stoff für eine Doku-Fiction, ein Genre, das seinem paradoxen Programm nach seine permanente Selbstauflösung in den Handlungen der Schauspieler, im Kopf des Regisseurs und in der Fernbedienung der Zuschauer gleich mitbetreibt. Auflösung ist das Stichwort, die eigentlich treibende Form des Romans, und Flametti und mit ihm seine Frau stemmen sich beharrlich über alle haarfein geschilderten Abgründigkeiten gegen eine solche. Eine Kopfwehtablette, sprudelnd im halbleeren Wasserglas, in Endlosschleife wäre das ein Bild. Das Leben ist nicht einfach, und das hat auch keiner behauptet. Und wenn Flamingo Mehmed nicht kassiert worden wäre, hätte man schon können … Das Geschehen in der Welt und in der Nacht dieser Hasardeure besticht durch sein verzweifeltes Bemühen um Struktur in der Grimasse einer Welt der rigorosen Beliebigkeit, einem Durchhaltewillen, dessen Durchhalteparolen schon deshalb von weit her klingen, weil von Anbeginn an klar ist, dass Durchhalten keinen Ausnahmezustand, sondern die Regel bedeutet. Dazu kommt, dass eigentlich keiner der Akteure etwas kann oder wirklich so gut kann, dass damit „Staat zu machen" wäre. Richtiger Erfolg auf einer richtigen Bühne muss ein Traum bleiben, schon um wenigstens dieses Klischee auf Horizont zu halten. Was bleibt, ist die zusammengebastelte Nummernrevue, und welch Glück, dass das Wort „Revue" zugleich für das Programm auf der Bühne wie für die Zeitschrift steht, die vereint, was überall sonst auch nicht zusammenpasst. Zwischen Revue und Flugblatt wird die Aufführungsform von DADA als permanente Ankündigung verhandelt.

Flamingos leben in seichten Gewässern. Sie können ihren Hals bedenklich verbiegen und ihren Schnabel als Reuse für Kleinstlebewesen nutzen. Sie bekommen ihre verführerische Farbe nur, wenn sie die entsprechende Nahrung zu sich nehmen, und wenn diese ausbleibt, sind sie zwar nur halbrosa, aber zur Not geht das auch. Sie stehen gerne auf einem Bein, und eifrige Biologen fügen schnell hinzu, man stünde dann stabiler – im Wasser, im Matsch, vielleicht.

Tal R hat mit *Flamingo Flametti* eine plausible Alliteration vorgelegt, die nicht unbedingt auf der Hand lag. Und was er als Installationskünstler, der sich schon gar nicht auf Genrefragen einlässt, dann unter diesem Label zusammenbringt, schuldet der Revue zumindest das Konzept der sinnfälligen Reihung, die gerne so, aber auch anders aussehen könnte. Dass Emmy Hennings im Varieté Glock in der Aeschenvorstadt in Basel mit Flamingo und seinem Maxim-Ensemble als Kopf einer Spinne auftrat, ist kein Zufall, sondern schon die Zugabe. Das Prinzip, Dinge im Raum zueinander in Beziehung zu bringen, ist dem Geschwisterpaar Montage und Konstellation zu verdanken, und wir können uns bei diesem eineiigen Zwilling, *les deux sœurs*, nicht entscheiden, welche wir mehr lieben. Die provozierte Herausbildung von „Resten" im Studio, das bekanntermaßen ein Paradies ist, hat mit der Zuweisung von Wert als einem Teil des Ganzen zu tun. Jede Installation, ob *Flamingo Flametti* oder *Mann über Bord*, wird so zur Rekonstruktion einer wunderbaren Welt, die es im Studio fast einmal gegeben hätte. Das Studio bleibt das natürliche Habitat des Flamingos. Es ist sein See, sein Étang de Vaccarès. Jede Neuaufstellung der Elemente, so verschieden oder so ähnlich sie sich sein mögen, ergibt eine neue Konstellation, eine Variation der Wiederholung für nur einen Moment. Das Morgen sieht anders aus. Ihre Struktur kommt uns als mit leichter Hand gebaute Anti-Ökonomie entgegen; im Tausch der Wörter für ihre Bezeichnung, dem Tausch der Gesten für ihre Benutzung, manche drehen sich selbst um die eigene Achse und wie von Wunderhand getrieben, andere erzeugen Töne in ihrem Inneren. Der *Concrete Tape Recorder*, der immer noch sendet. Flamingo Moore *bound to fail*, Flamingo Jolly Roger, Flamingo Roger Moore in *Der Spion, der mich liebte*.

Flamingo Tal wirft alle Bälle gleichzeitig in die Luft. Alle Elemente sind in diesem Moment Wesen. Sie können ihrer Bedeutung nach, ihrer Morphologie nach und sogar ihrer phonetischen Erscheinungsweise nach fließend ineinander übergehen. Es gibt fantastische Willkür als Programm. Die Konstellation *Flamingo Flametti* präsentiert nichts als reale oder imaginäre Wirklichkeit. Sie ist pure Imagination im gleichen Augenblick, wie sie die Modelle ihrer Wirklichkeit aussetzt, so lange, bis sie schließlich zum Modell für sich selbst wird, was wieder auf anderes als Modell angewendet werden kann – wie einst DADA. Nicht als feste Form, nicht als Ding an sich, als Kunstwerk für die, die es so wollen, als Requisiten für den Einsatz jetzt. Die Flaggen dienen keinem Semaphor-Alphabet, keiner kennt den Code. Eintritt frei, die eigentliche Illusion. Der Auftrag heißt Wind, nicht Richtung.

— Axel Heil

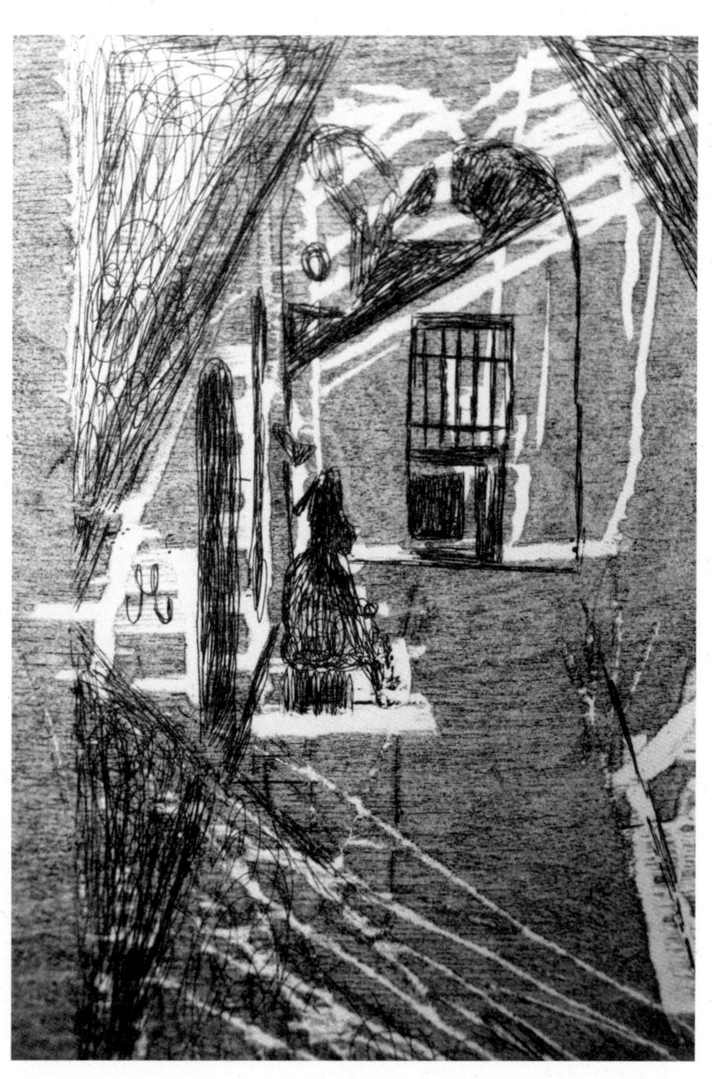

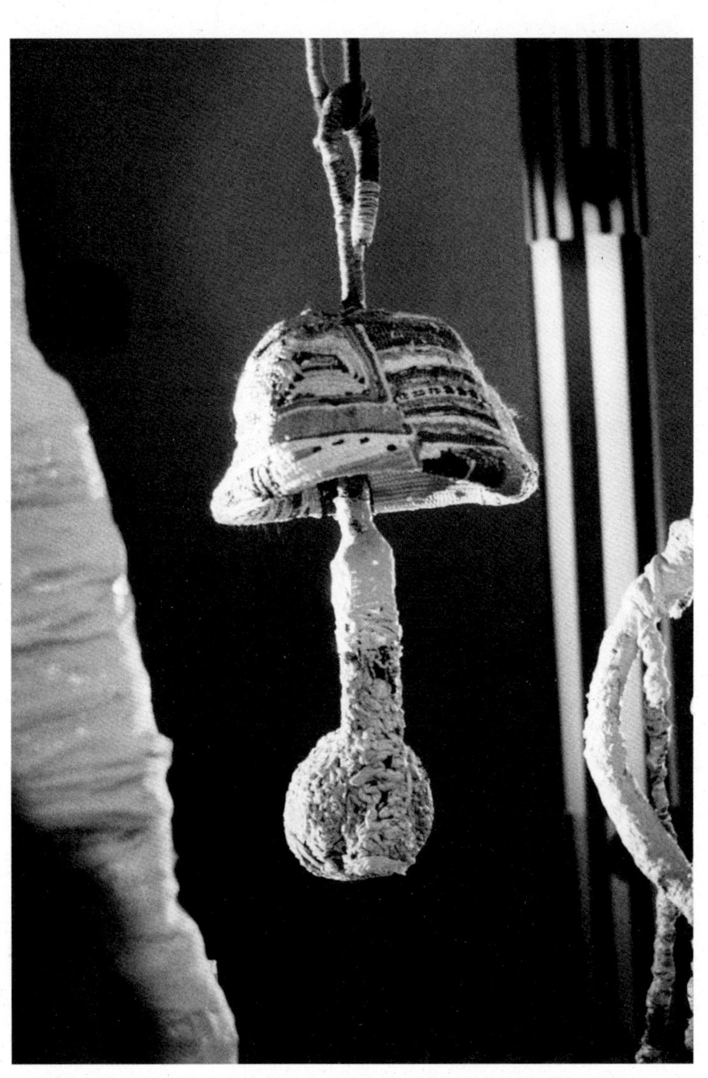

CLEAN-UP OPERATIONS

It was in the middle of summer 1958 with the *DADA* exhibition that the Kunstverein für die Rheinlande und Westfalen in Dusseldorf organised the first institutional clean-up operation of a European legend that had occurred forty years previously. The museum, disguised as an action, tried, by avoiding experiments, to salvage the fragments of a movement and put them back together in such a way that out of the haphazard and individual pieces, an ordered whole governed by the law of chance could emerge – a promising venture. The form of action was not 'combine' but 'patch up'. It was not about collage but glue. The keywords of reconstruction were soon at the ready in the jargon of the time: 'rampant new shoots on the growth of modern art', 'contortions worthy of a sideshow', 'advertising-obsessed slapstick', 'a demonstration of silly childish behaviour' or even the all-encompassing 'questionable nonsense'.

The ground-breaking MoMA exhibition, which covered the wider spectrum between *Fantastic art, Dada and Surrealism* in 1936, and even more so Robert Motherwell's monograph *The Dada painters and poets*, which was widely celebrated in artistic circles, are only remembered by a handful of people in the republic of the *Wirtschaftswunder* [economic miracle] – the initiated of a small circle of 'those who were involved'. Everything else was first of all propaganda from the wrong side, which faced another kind of art with different criteria full of incomprehension. It was a small group which not only wanted to put DADA back in the minds but wanted to (and could) conjure up 'the other tradition' at the dawn of the 1960s. DADA as the success of the history of its reception in Europe begins here.

DIE YOUNG STAY PRETTY

Many of the original Dadaists were still alive, and the fact that in the haze of the Adenauer era they could at least be addressed as survivors of the modern art movement had less to do with their works than their frequently nomadic existence and lives dictated by endless disruption. Arp, Man Ray, Ribemont-Dessaignes, Max Ernst, Hannah Höch, Huelsenbeck, Tzara, Hausmann, Hans Richter and Duchamp were still alive. Schwitters, Picabia, Ball, Emmy Hennings and Sophie Taeuber had long since gone to the happy hunting grounds. Even though these artists appear just as shadows in this exhibition, all their anticipated objections and contradictions and their 'Columbus did not discover America' attitude let DADA '58 as 'a mindset' sail off into the open sea disguised as a ship, a raft. To explain this phenomenon the organisers of the exhibition cling on the islands familiar to them, from DADA Zurich to DADA New York, from DADA Paris to DADA Berlin. And in an act of desperation, with heavy heart, they reach for the word 'movement'. The artists let this pass, they are older now and all are happy to tell the best story from their youth. Hausmann wrote laconically from Limoges: "This movement has made significant contributions to the psychology of the individual and the masses, as of the visual artist and the poet." Max Ernst is already annoyed when, during a game of boules with his old playmate Patrick Waldberg in the equally rural Huismes, he says: "I know, I know, a DADA exhibition. Another one! What is it with all these people that they want to make DADA into a museum piece?"And then, in plain language: "DADA was a bomb". And finally, "It is the advantage of DADA to have died young."

KO IN THE FOURTH ROUND

Flamingo Fernande also did not tire of telling stories about her great times, the years spent on the little hill overlooking Paris, the *butte* of Montmartre, just after the turn of the century and before the Great War. Casually complacent is the story that Flamingo Pablo was particularly proud of, that he and his entourage, the *'bande à Picasso'*, all unknown poets and unfortunate painters wandering aimlessly in some parts of the *quartier*, were mistaken for a gang of boxers. That was better than being an artist – at least potentially dangerous. Flamingo Cravan managed to bridge the gap between poet and boxer professionally, even when everyone knew that Flamingo Gauguin, when it came to it, was always up for a fight, and Flamingo Braque worked on his feared left hook into old age. Cravan lost in Barcelona to the heavyweight world champion *el gran* Jack Johnson, and it was a true fight. KO in the sixth round – it paid for his passage to New York.

In their anti-ideological struggle against tradition and for a 'different modern art', the Flamingos immediately encountered some bizarre problems. How could the silly distinction between fortunate play and sense of responsibility, and even more so the dilemma of a radical critique of the 'destruction of the world', simultaneously holding on to a romantically coloured ideal, be reconciled? How can 'successful and genuine art', considered as 'form and process', be incorporated into a continually moving action that must permanently be renegotiated? Where was the thing that in the end was 'not art' but could still pass off as a kick that made life bearable, or at least helped to want to carry on living. Was it already asking too much to regard 'the poetry of day-to-day life' as the real manifestation of art, and to regard its result, the highly praised artwork of the individual genius, as an obsolete relic, a remnant? Is playing chess akin to art? Is every watercolour bigger than a hand akin to sport? Where were the yardsticks which allowed one to make a clear judgement, and where was the audience, which would at least be prepared to support these lower echelons of a weary civilisation?

A few pennies to enter the world of the circus, but they can be found can't they? The theatrical prop which only appears when 'it' is being used and which is regarded as nothing more than a cast-off tool later in the evening and between performances, an 'artefact' for something that can also be used by different actors in different ways. It seemed to be a way out and 60 years later, Flamingo Franz West would refer to it as *Passstück*, an 'adaptive'. It is the reverse idea of the *objet trouvé*: it is the lost object, the object that disappears after the tour and casually ends up in the concierge's attic or is never found again. Initially putting the prop on a 'pedestal' helps it, and throughout history we learn that the shipping crate and its accompanying inventory determine the provisional finale. Flamingo Picabia discovers the model for the *Portrait d'une jeune fille americaine dans l'état de nudité* [Portrait of an American girl in a state of nudity] at an ironmonger, and Duchamp, the bicycle wheel. Today we also know that *So ein Ding will ich auch haben* [I also want to have such a thing] and *Fill with own imagination* help us get through difficult times.

THE SKIN OF THE BEAR

In 1915, in the Munich home of the wealthy collector Herta Koenig, Rainer Maria Rilke sat opposite a picture that Koenig had recently secured from the avant-garde art dealer Thannhauser, who had acquired it on the eve of the First World War in Paris, at the auction of an art fund with the pretentious and metaphorical name of *The skin of the bear*. Not only in terms of size, it was the most important work by Picasso to have been sold at the time, and the price achieved at the public auction not only brought the investors a fabulous profit and the critics a serious theme, but above all brought the artist attention, renown and even a share of the profits. With a great deal of fanfare, Flamingo Picasso had started to develop his programmatic picture in the summer of 1905, and from the very outset, the *Family of Saltimbanques* was considered 'more' than the backstage portrayal of a family of artists. In Rilke's fifth Duino elegy, we then have the highly dramatic lines:

But WHO *are* they, tell me, these travellers, even more /
transient than we are ourselves, urgently, from their earliest days, /
wrung out for *whom* – to please *whom*, / by a never-satisfied will?

In the line structure, the portrayal of the acrobats – "an old man, only a drummer now" and "the young one, the man, as if he were son of a neck and a nun" as far as the "seldom affectionate mother" – breathes heavily, and the next performance is the most difficult, and the winter quarters have not yet been arranged. The artist's much-vaunted fascination for the circus and variety performance is so embedded in the stereotype of marginal existence in society, that the boundaries remain blurred even today – is it the poetry, the method or the metaphors that are conjuring up the form?

SLACKLINE

Giovanni Domenico was Tiepolo's son, and along with his brother Lorenzo, he was involved in his father's gigantic art projects from a very early age. That *'les deux frères'* themselves would inevitably become painters is shown by the implicit nature of the mundane transfer of a thriving family business as the inheritance of genius and social class. As a legend, it reflects a fate that is just as inevitable as the story of the circus child who grows up in the sawdust of the ring and, with no alternative, therefore has to become a tightrope walker. The fact that the child is as thin as a rake but muscular, is both a blessing and a curse of his wrested existence. Here, the supposed ideal of beauty stems from hunger and takes us back to the same story of the *peintre maudit* who, out of desperation, throws those enchanting drawings of the tightrope walker with a tear in his eye into the fire so as not to freeze in winter. In Flamingo Tiepolo's picture *Pulcinella e i saltimbanchi*, the tightropes are lying on the ground, and in a foolhardy manner, the acrobats turn cartwheels in front of the astonished onlookers; it would be much easier without a tightrope. We owe the white costumes of the masked clowns to the stylised costumes of the *Commedia dell'arte*. Their costume includes a conical hat which bears an astonishing resemblance to the most famous photograph from the DADA era – Hugo Ball on the stage of the Cabaret Voltaire, Zurich in 1916. Flamingo Ball's improvised cardboard tube is more armour than costume, and even as a costume it is more a substitute costume. Sophie Taeuber, so as not to compromise her position as teacher at the Zurich Kunstgewerbeschule, always appeared on stage only 'in disguise' and wearing a mask. That she can be seen in one photo in full regalia with Janco's mask wearing the same arm warmers and false-finger paper gloves as Ball in the well-known image, suggests a varied use of some props but their not being assigned to any particular character on the DADA stage.

The public's reception of the press photo inevitably made Flamingo Ball the King of DADA, or at least an awkward bishop. In the hierarchy of the DADA universe there can be no concept of king or bishop, and universe is always too much, and universe is cheap, and it is only the contradictions that a photograph of the pseudo boss can develop over a period of one hundred years that remain interesting. Hugo Ball, with his frozen gestures, and no movement, stands as *the artist is present* at the beginning of DADA, and his clever self-stylisation already exudes perfection at a time when neither a proper beginning nor the word DADA as a label nor the term DADA as an exception to the much-tormented isms even existed. The audience increasingly liked the motif – it fits the label.

Am Anfang war das Wort Am [In the beginning was the word In], coined by Total-Flamingo Timm Ulrichs, a joker who took himself and his actions seriously in a game in which he, where necessary, even marries Anna Blume who, as is generally known, was always attracted to other Flamingos and still is. Emmy Hennings is 'Pretty Flamingo'.

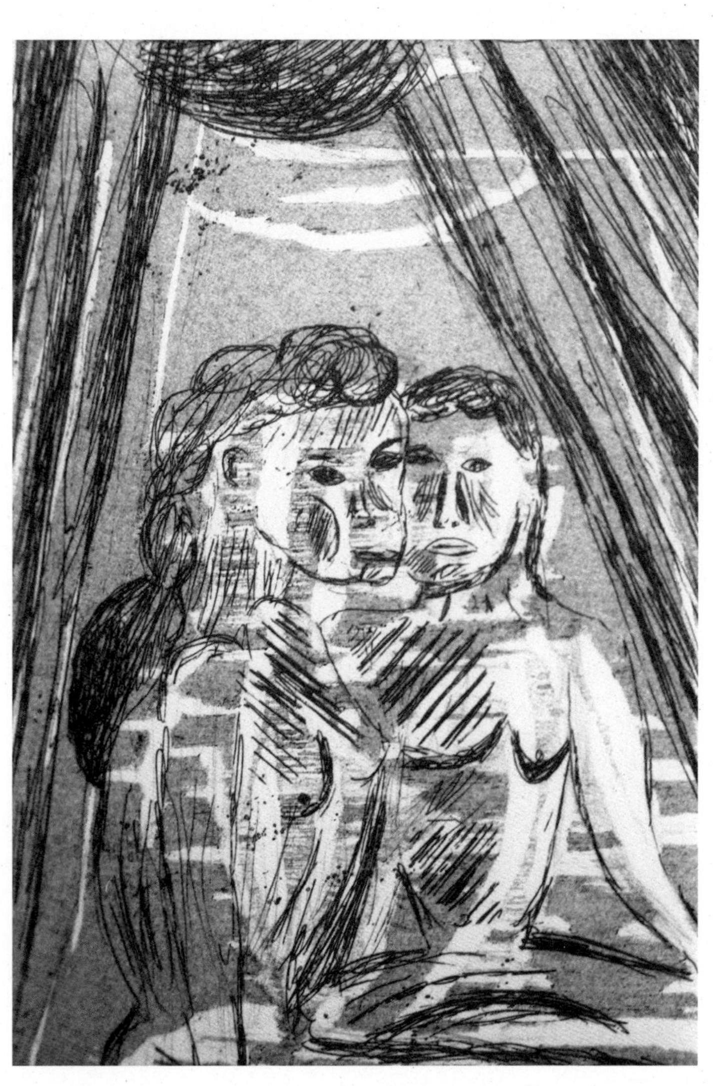

THE REAL FLAMETTI

The word DADA does not, of course, appear in Hugo Ball's work *Flametti oder Vom Dandysmus der Armen* [Flametti or the dandyism of the poor]. It is a novel which does little to hide the milieu and the obstinately organised yet strangely aimless existence of a variety performance company as its theme, but whose allusions to living persons are otherwise negotiated as a purely coincidental and obviously unintentional part of the plot. Today, *Flametti* is certainly the stuff of docu-fiction, a genre in which, in accordance with its paradoxical agenda, permanent self-dissolution is evoked by the actors' actions, the mind of the director, and the audience's remote control. Dissolution is the keyword, the driving force behind the novel whose subtly depicted atrocities Flametti and his wife doggedly try to resist. A headache tablet fizzing in a half-empty glass of water – in a continuous loop that would be a metaphor. Life is not easy, and no-one has maintained that it is. And if Flamingo Mehmed had not been nicked, it would have been possible to... What happens in the world and in the night of this gambler is captivating through its desperate attempt at structure in the grimace of a world of rigorous arbitrariness, a perseverance whose motivating words can be heard from afar because it is clear from the very beginning that perseverance is not the exception but the rule. Furthermore, none of the protagonists is capable of doing anything or capable of doing anything so well that there would be 'something to write home about'. Real success on a real stage must remain a dream, at least to keep this stereotype on the horizon. What remains is a cobbled-together revue, and what a stroke of luck that this word can refer to a stage programme and a newspaper which unites things that do not necessarily belong together. Between revue and leaflet, DADA's performance style is negotiated as a permanent announcement.

Flamingos live in shallow water. They can bend their necks in an alarming manner and use their beaks as a creel for microorganisms. They only acquire their seductive colour when they take in the appropriate food, and if this is lacking they are only half pink, but that's OK too. They like to stand on one leg, and enthusiastic biologists are quick to add that this makes them more stable – in water, in mud... perhaps.

With *Flamingo Flametti*, Tal R offers a plausible alliteration which is not necessarily obvious. And what he, as an installation artist who does not get involved with issues of genre at all, then brings together under this label, owes at least the concept of obvious sequence to the revue, a sequence that can readily be organised like this, or differently. That Emmy Hennings performed at the Varieté Glock in the Aeschenvorstadt in Basel with the real Flamingo and his Maxim-Ensemble as the head of a spider is no coincidence but an added bonus. We owe the principle of relating things to each other in space to the siblings of montage and constellation, and we cannot decide which of these identical twins, these *deux sœurs*, we like more. The provoked development of 'remnants' in the studio, that is known to be a paradise, has something to do with the assignment of value as a part of the whole. Every installation, whether *Flamingo Flametti* or *Mann über Bord* [Man overboard], thus becomes a reconstruction of 'the wonderful world that almost was' in the studio. The studio is the flamingo's natural habitat. It is his lake, his Étang de Vaccarès. Each new installation of the elements, as different or similar as they may be, results in a new constellation, a fleeting variation of the repetition. The following day it might look different. The structure appears to us as an anti-economy built with a light touch, with a change of words for its name, a change of gestures for its use, some turn on their own axis as if driven by a magic hand, and others generate sounds internally. The *Concrete Tape Recorder*, which is still transmitting. Flamingo Moore *bound to fail*, Flamingo Jolly Roger, Flamingo Roger Moore in *The spy who loved me*.

Flamingo Tal throws all the balls into the air at the same time. In this moment, all elements are beings. Depending on their meaning, their morphology and even their phonetic frequency, they can flow seamlessly into one another. There is fantastical randomness as a programme. The *Flamingo Flametti* constellation presents nothing as real or fictive reality. It is pure imagination at the same time as it exposes the models to its reality, until it finally becomes a model to itself, which in turn can be applied as a model for something else – like DADA once did. Not as a solid form, not as a thing per se, but as an artwork for those who want it to be an artwork, as props to be used now. The flags do not serve as a semaphore alphabet – nobody knows the code. Admission free, the true illusion. The commission is called wind, not direction.

— Axel Heil

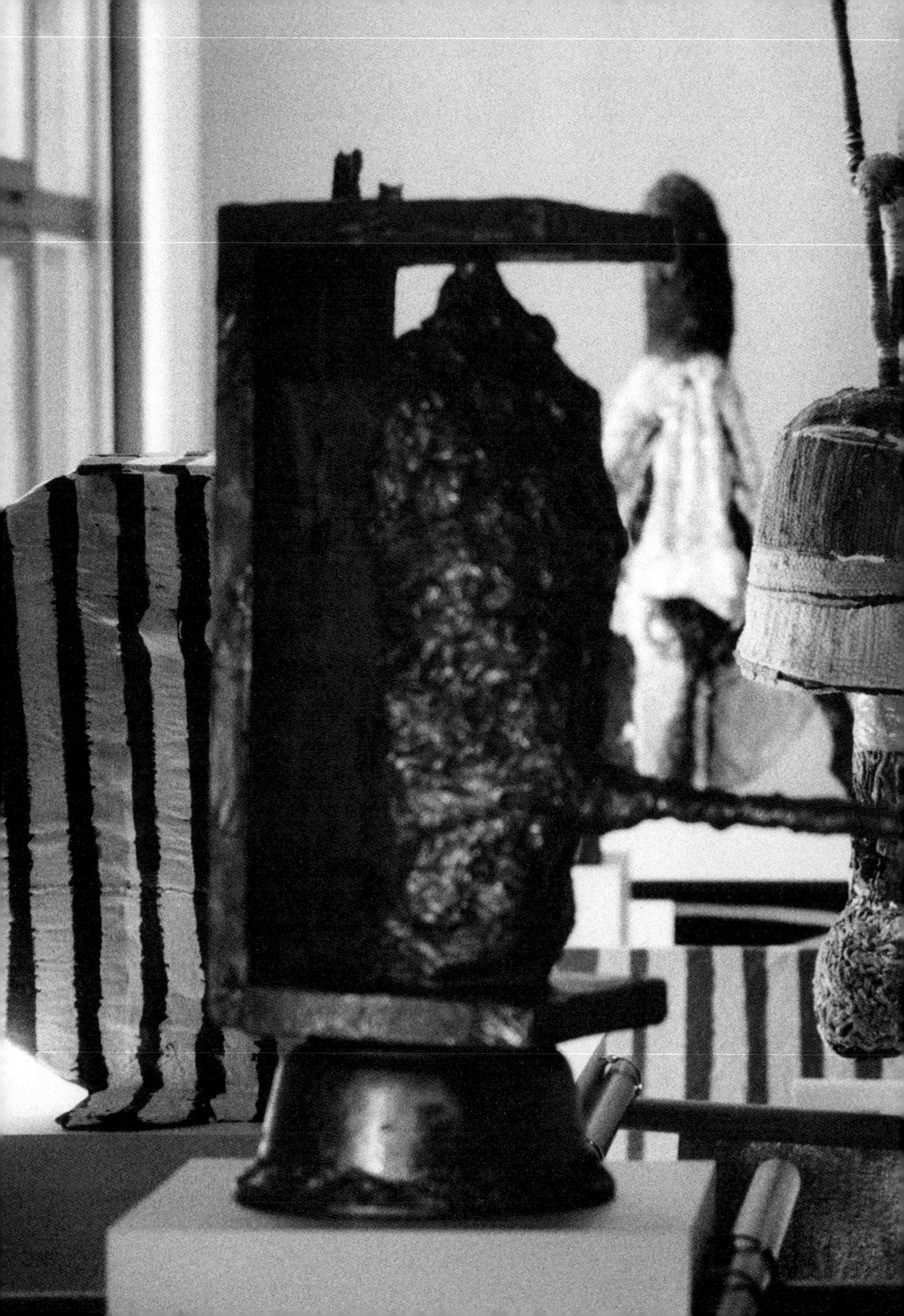

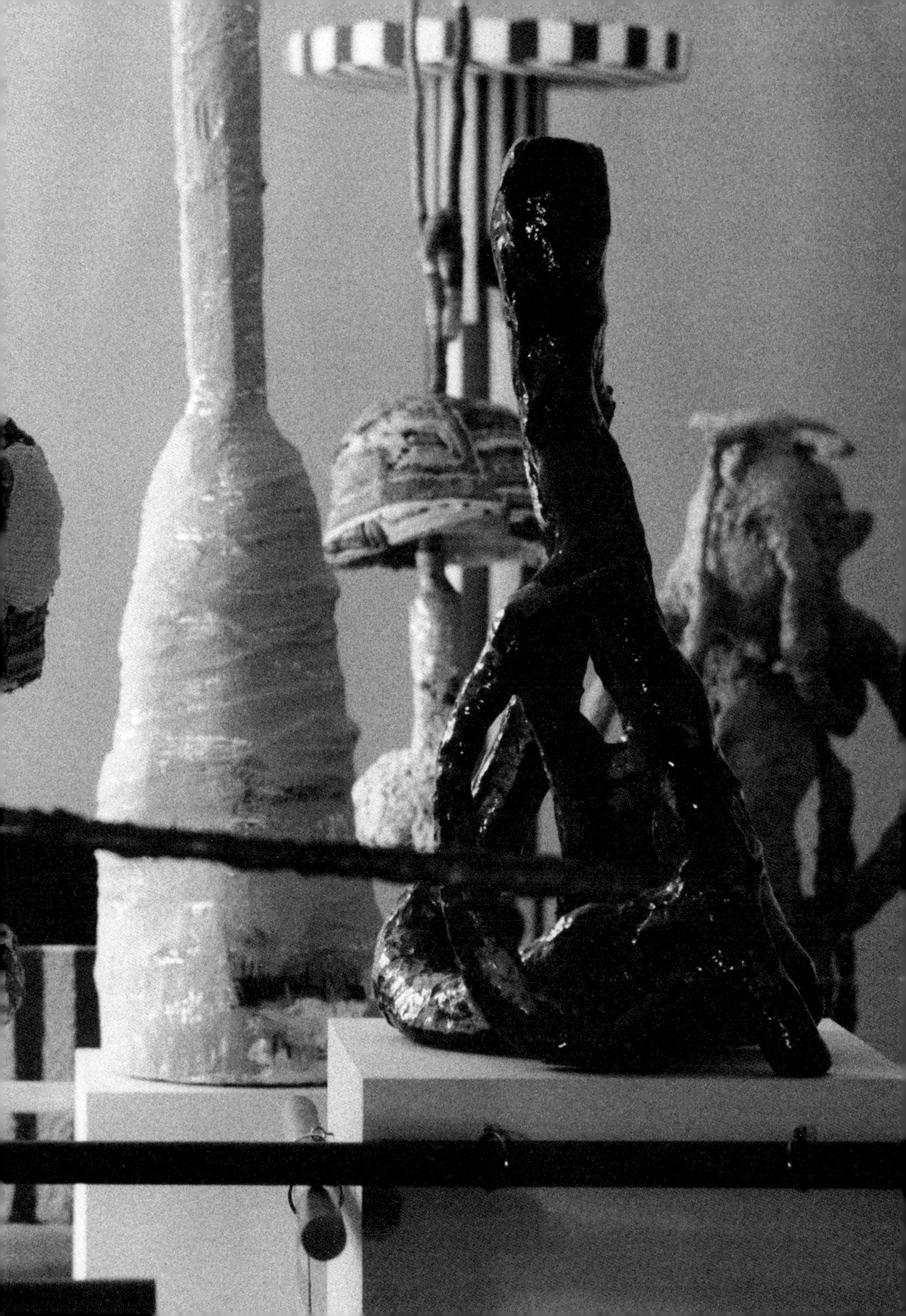

EXHIBITED WORKS

Tal R

"The Navigator", 2012
natural bronze
83 × 115 × 33 cm
On turning plinth

"Chimney", 2013
PVC plywood foam and
printed fabric
214 × 75 × 75 Ø 75 cm
On turning plinth

"Chimney", 2013
PVC plywood foam and
printed fabric
162 × 60 × 60 Ø 60 cm

"The Somali", 2014
plastic toys, wood, wire, yarn,
soft cement, aluminium foil,
aluminium paint, acrylic
124 × 78 × 62 cm

"Sonntag", 2014
acrylic, found objects,
wood and yarn
121 × 30 × 62 cm

"Cloud", 2013 – 2014
bronze
114 × 80 × 44 cm

"Snow Walk", 2015
aluminium
62 × 68 × 53 cm

"Obstacle", 2015
acrylic, black board paint,
cardboard, fabric, glue and wood
95 × 178 × 40 cm

"Trojan", 2015
acrylic, black board paint, papier-
mâché, silver leaf and wood
82 × 224 × 35 cm

"Scholars Palace", 2015
raku fired ceramic
96 × 52 × 48 cm

"Schwester Fanta", 2015
acrylic, aluminium paint, asphalt
paint, fabric, found objects,
plaster, glue rag gugs, silver leaf,
string and wood
182 × 202 × 43 cm
On turning plinth

"Owl", 2015
acrylic, cardboard, fabric,
plaster, glue and wood
72 × 92 × 63 cm

"House X", 2015
acrylic, black board paint,
cardboard, fabric, plaster,
glue and wood
46 × 52 × 53 cm

Exhibition poster:
"Flamingo Flametti", 2016
woodcut
72 × 100 cm
Edition of 18
printed by Michael Schäfer,
Copenhagen

Flags:
"Eel", "Flamingo", "Abjure",
"Mehmed", "Indians", "Flyinfish
Sehhorses", "Flametti", "Saal",
"Flamin", "Vowel", "Turk", "Inn"
wood, cardboard, acrylic
75 × 132 cm

Sarah Bogner

Vaudeville Zebra, 2016
Sound installation
23:11 min (loop)

Axel Heil

"eine Sekunde stumm staunen
(für Emmy Hennings)", 2016
Montrage with works by
Jean Arp, Georges Brassaï, Ernst
Moritz Engert, Max Ernst, Raoul
Hausmann, Emmy Hennings, Willi
Müller-Hufschmid, Francis Picabia,
Kurt Schwitters, Tristan Tzara
250 × 350 cm

Josef Zekoff

"H. B. + E. H. – Spiegelgasse 1916",
2016
wood, paper, artistprint
64 × 64 × 180 cm

WORKS

Original prints by TAL R from the
artist's book "Flametti oder vom
Dandysmus der Armen"

"Flametti in the Corner", 2013
woodcut / etching
24 × 33 cm (detail)
page 47

"Flametti", 2013
woodcut / etching
24 × 33 cm (detail)
page 50

"Mehmed in Jail", 2013
woodcut / etching
24 × 33 cm (detail)
page 53

"Two Young Fräulein", 2013
woodcut / etching
24 × 33 cm (detail)
page 59

IMPRINT

Flamingo Flametti
Tal R, Axel Heil, Harpune Wien

Editor: Sarah Bogner and
Josef Zekoff, Harpune Wien
Text: Axel Heil
Design: Raphael Drechsel, GREAT
Translation (from German into
English): Catherine Schelbert,
Andrea Stettler
Proofreading: Martina Buder
Photos: Josef Zekoff
Print: Holzhausen Druck GmbH

Published and distributed by
VfmK Verlag für moderne Kunst
GmbH, www.vfmk.org

ISBN 978-3-903131-25-5

The book is coming out on
the occasion of the "Flamingo
Flametti" exhibition.

A review of the artist's book
"Flametti oder vom Dandysmus
der Armen" by Tal R and Hugo Ball
with Harpune Wien and Axel
Heil at the Zumikon – Institut für
moderne Kunst Nürnberg,
Feb. 4 – April 2, 2016

See also: Hugo Ball, "Flametti
oder vom Dandysmus der Armen"
artist's book by Tal R with 10
original prints in an edition of 30
from Harpune Verlag, 2013

English paperback edition Hugo
Ball, "Flametti or the Dandyism
of the Poor" illustrated by Tal R,
first translation by Catherine
Schelbert, Wakefield Press, 2014

BUNDESKANZLERAMT ▪ ÖSTERREICH

Thanks to:

Karen Bjelke, Friedrich Brandstetter,
Margrit Brehm, Veronika Breit,
Sofia Fischer, Tusnelda Frellesvig,
Julia Grevenkamp, Silvia Jaklitsch,
Volker Koch, Anton Lebhard, Marc
Lowenthal, Allan Lyth, Paradis,
Christina Petutschnigg, Manfred
Rothenberger, Michael Schäfer,
Catherine Schelbert, Elfie Semotan,
Jens Stampe, Petra Weigle, Marietta
and Kurt Zein